ALL THAT JAZZ AND MORE...
The Complete Book of Jazz Dancing

A publication of
Leisure Press.
597 Fifth Avenue; New York, N.Y. 10017
Copyright © 1983 Leisure Press
All rights reserved. Printed in the U.S.A.

No part of this publication may be reproduced
or transmitted in any form or by any means
electronic or mechanical, including photocopying, recording,
or any information storage and retrieval system now known
or to be invented, without permission in writing from the publisher,
except by a reviewer who wishes to quote brief passages
in connection with a written review for
inclusion in a magazine, newspaper, or broadcast.

Library of Congress Catalog Card Number: 82-83944

ISBN: 0-88011-124-0

Cover design: Brian Groppe
Book design: Diana J. Goodin
Typesetting: The Graphics Connection; Oakland, California

ALL THAT JAZZ AND MORE...
The Complete Book of Jazz Dancing

CHRISTY LANE
Photography by GENE ROCKEY

A Must For Teachers and Students Of Jazz Dance, Performing Arts, Gymnastics, Physical Education, Pep Squads, Skating, and Aerobic Dance.

Attire furnished by the Dressing Room
Spokane, WA

Hair designs by Kathy Lunke

LEISURE PRESS
New York

CONTENTS

Acknowledgements 7

Introduction 9

1 *JAZZ DANCE TODAY* 11
2 *THE JAZZ CLASS* 13
3 *GETTING READY* 14
4 *BASIC JAZZ POSITIONS* 16
5 *CENTER FLOOR EXERCISE TECHNIQUE* 39
6 *FLOOR EXERCISE TECHNIQUE* 58
7 *ISOLATION EXERCISE TECHNIQUE* 90
8 *KICKS (BATTEMENTS)* 108
9 *LOCOMOTIVE MOVEMENTS* 126
10 *FLOORWORK* 167
11 *TURNS* 180
12 *PUTTING IT ALL TOGETHER—CHOREOGRAPHY* 206
13 *NOW DANCE IT!* 209
14 *ROUTINES* 211
15 *S-T-R-E-T-C-H-ABILITY* 222
16 *THE DANCER AS AN ATHLETE* 231
17 *FOR TEACHERS ONLY* 233

Suggested Readings 236

Index 237

ACKNOWLEDGEMENTS

I am indebted to all the students and teachers for their inspiration to compel me to write this book. Their questions and encouragement led me to finish these studies.

I am most grateful to Maxine Davis whose final "kick" gave me the impetus to write this book.

I thank my friends, Gene and Lee Rockey, Linda Eckhardt, Kathy Lunke, Susan Perron, Jeri Thomas, Tom Edson, Charlene Sherlock, Judy Crabb, Terrence Rockey, and dancers Chris Anderson, Isabelle Cook, Beth Failing, Shawna Berens, Lisa Jackson, and Mike Anderson for their assistance and support in my project.

My appreciation is extended to Oregon State University Basketball program and Eastern Washington University for use of their facilities and equipment.

Dedicated to my mother and father, Eleanor and Nicholas, for giving me life so I can experience and enjoy this wonderful art.

And to Jerry for sharing it with me.

INTRODUCTION

Eight has always been a lucky number to me. It was eight years ago that I received my first letter of inquiry from a desparate jazz dance instructor pleading for literature on the subject of jazz dance. From that time on, I began traveling nationally and the letters continued to come. Where did I get my material? What's the basic technique and how can I teach the progressions? These inquiries, plus my own curiosity, caused me to seek a universal technique and approach to studying and teaching jazz dance. My ambition was not to become a professional performing dancer, but rather to learn more about the art form that I came to love. And my enjoyment and satisfaction in teaching have led me to these findings of sound jazz dance technique.

Being one of those fortunate few who had the opportunity to travel in forty-two states teaching and training at workshops, I searched for common denominators in instruction that would meet the needs of students and teachers alike. From New York to Los Angeles, I saw many very different styles, techniques and philosophies, not only in private dance studios, but in private gymnastics clubs, high schools, colleges, universities, YMCA's, dance caravans and conventions. One thing was obvious wherever I went, jazz dancing could turn an empty room into excitement, energy and beauty.

This study is the product of extensive research in the field; from writings, films, classes taken from masters, observation of professional choreographers as well as my own classes including the special master workshops where many techniques were tested. I've written this book in an attempt to standardize the basics. The arrangement is unique in that it is designed for the novice as well as the advanced. It will be an asset to anyone involved in jazz dance today, whether you are a dancer, teacher, choreographer, actor or actress, athlete or just an aerobics fan—there's something here for you. And let us not exclude the physical education instructors who are dedicating so much of their effort and time building programs in their schools and keeping up with the demands of dance in the curriculum. This book is especially for those teachers in the educational setting.

Whatever your interest or perspective, I invite you to join me in the exciting adventure of jazz dance.

1 Jazz Dance Today

Welcome to the world of jazz dance; whether you are a novice student, an advanced student, or especially if you are a teacher! This book is designed to inform you, stimulate you, enhance your technique and improve your control in the wonderful art of jazz dance.

When you think of jazz, you probably think of the lindy hop, jitterbug, swing, musical comedy or Blacks doing the Charleston in the twenties. Maybe you think of Fred Astaire or Gene Kelly dancing in the thirties. The eighties, however, have produced much more. Jazz dance has now begun to regard itself as an art. No longer is it done exclusively to jazz music, but performed to pop, rhythm, blues, rock and disco as well. Never has jazz dance been so popular as today. Everywhere people are gathering in classes in increasing numbers for more than just fitness. Fun, excitement, challenge, entertainment, sporty, artistic and self-expression are all descriptions of jazz dance used by jazz enthusiasts.

Jazz dance is also being used as a means of communication through our present audiovisual media. It is available through many channels of our culture—the theatre, movies, television commercials and variety shows—and is the most widely viewed dance form in the United States. It's literally everywhere—in night club acts, sports entertainment, gymnastics routines, pep squad routines, skating routines and now it's influencing the aerobics world. Jazz dance is even spreading from college curriculums to secondary school classes as well.

Why is it so popular? Aside from the media influence and pure enjoyment, jazz dance is a natural form of dance that is freer, more exciting, more rhythmic and less classical than other dance forms. This dance form teaches the body to move rhythmically while challenging the mind with patterned movement. It can develop muscle tone, reduce fatigue, psychologically release tension and build self-confidence by giving you the feeling you have control over your body.

Perhaps the best thing about jazz dance is that it is contemporary, always grasping the new while clinging on to yesterday. Through the other disciplines of dance we have created the versatile jazz that is seen today. During the past decade jazz has adapted material from artistic, social and theatrical dance forms. For example, ballet has contributed to jazz by giving it exactness and alignment (not to mention those French words!). The nearly concurrent influence of modern dance has given it greater use of the torso, natural expression and more fluidity. Tap dance has brought rhythmic movement, terminology and speed. Gymnastics has provided flexibility, suppleness and strength. From folk, ballroom and social dance we see step patterns while character dance provides versatility. As a result of the "melting pot" nature of America, we are now seeing many cultural influences. And of course, contemporary dances—such as rock, soul and disco have stimulated jazz with progressive styles that utilize a variety of movements of the hips and torso.

It is obviously apparent that a great many influences have shaped the jazz of today. Due to this, jazz has developed many styles that if named could be categorized as follows: Jazz Ballet (a lyrical style with many ballet movements); Modern Jazz (more fluid style with greater torso movement), Rock Jazz (current contemporary dances utilizing much hip movement intertwined with jazz), Broadway Musical Jazz (musical show production dancing), Afro-Jazz (jazz influenced with African cultural movements), and Latin Jazz (emphasis on hip movements and a 1-2-3 rhythm).

Now let's turn to jazz dance and its value to you, the reader. As you read this book, you will explore jazz techniques and terminology that is used in all the above mentioned styles of jazz. However, we will not go into all the ballet, modern, social and cultural movements that some of the styles use heavily. We will leave these dance moves to those who are the experts in that area. We will, however, use some of the terms and movements that are quite prominent in all the styles.

From Los Angeles to New York there are a great many different performers and teachers from their own backgrounds, all putting forth their own techniques. Through this influence, a universal technique—a common denominator—has emerged. You are about to learn this technique.

2 THE JAZZ CLASS

It seems we have accepted ideas for dance today based on traditions developed hundreds of years ago in Europe. That was a time when the art was likely to be ritualistic and geometric rather than realistic or humanistic. The dance techniques that were written then were developed by people who knew a great deal less about the human body than is known today. As society's awareness of the anatomical and kinesiological parameters of the human body has increased, jazz classes have changed to accommodate the needs and demands of the human body. It's wonderful that with the recent fitness explosion has come concern for the personal safety of the dancer and more realistic approaches to dance.

From coast to coast, the jazz dance class still follows basically the same format as the traditional ballet class: 1) *exercise technique* for conditioning and control; 2) *locomotive movement* technique for balance and control; and 3) *combinations* or routines. In a professional studio, the average minimum amount of class time is one hour for beginners and 1½ hours for advanced students. An average intermediate class includes the following schedule: approximately thirty minutes of standing, floor, and isolation exercise techniques, twenty-five minutes of turns and locomotive moves (walks, jumps, floorwork); and twenty minutes on dance combinations or routines. More recently, studio work also includes a brief "warm-down" consisting of stretches, deep breathing, or a slow adage routine. Of course the time allotment for each section may vary. For example, a teacher may want to spend more time on a technique at the beginning of the term and more time on routines when getting close to performance time.

Today, teachers and dancers are placing a greater emphasis on exercise techniques designed to develop control, muscular strength, flexibility and coordination of all body parts. Thus, dancers are more effective and seem to have fewer injuries. Rather than just developing the "lines" of a dancer as was once done, individuals are concerned with training a dancer's body until it becomes completely and instantly responsive. Such exercises are a *must* in a class since they teach discipline and placement and if performed correctly, gradually give dancers the ability to achieve a balanced and integrated control of their movements. The exercises also increase the temperature of the connective tissues and make them not only less vulnerable to injury, but also more receptive to the lasting benefits of stretch during movement.

Some teachers include a "barre" exercise section in their class work. The "barre" is a term used for opening exercises done using a wall bar for balance. I have not included a barre section in this book since I do not feel that barre work is essential. Performing the exercises *without* the barre encourages full muscle usage, eliminates dependency on a support system and keeps you from attempting movements you are not prepared to accomplish effectively. However, if you wish, all the exercises listed in the Center Floor Chapter can be done at the barre.

Very common in classes today is an exercise routine or "adage." In adage, teachers choreograph a standardized slow series of center floor movements. These movements are performed as though without effort, but are a definite test of balance, control and strength. They also are a test of movement memory. These exercises must be done technically "clean," i.e., with a high degree of precision. Routines allow the dancer to memorize the movements, thus requiring less concentration on succeeding movements, and more concentration on placement, corrections, and "dancing" the exercise. A routine gives the freedom to "feel" the body and use the counts thoroughly rather than just going through the motions. It also allows the teacher to point out certain errors and achievements without stopping the music. Exercise routines are suggested for short periods of time. It is essential to vary the routine as the same exercises may limit the areas of the body being worked as well as become boring for both student and teacher.

In order to put together your own routine, try combining the exercises illustrated in the exercise technique chapters. Whether your workout is self-administered or with a teacher in class, spend a minimum of one-half of your workout time on either an adage combination or a complete exercise routine to include center floor, isolations and turns.

And, if you are attending a class where you feel the exercises are not warming up your body sufficiently, it is *your* responsibility to come to class early and do the work that is needed for you. Only you know your body, its condition and its limitations. Only try what your body is ready for and be a self-evaluator of the suggestions of others. Work on your weaknesses more than your strengths so you become a balanced dancer.

3 GETTING READY

Every exercise that is presented in this book is labeled either Level I (for beginning students), Level II (for intermediate students), or Level III (for advanced students) according to what I believe is appropriate. Obviously, Level I can be used by intermediate or advanced students and Level II can be used by advanced students. Keep in mind each studio or school has their own graded system according to the ability of the students enrolled.

Pay special attention to the technique chapters. Acquiring a sound technique is an investment in the future. Adherence to sound techniques frees your body to reach your ultimate potential. Once you've acquired the techniques, then you are ready to find the most exciting part of dancing—developing your own style.

Remember, the importance of proper breathing cannot be overemphasized. It is very easy to forget to breathe while one is executing a difficult skill! Never hold your breath while performing. Breathe deeply, naturally, and rhythmically and use your breathing to increase your energy. Breathing correctly will sharpen your concentration and add fluidness to your motions.

Proper attire is necessary in dance. There are many wonderful products on the market today. However, some can be extremely expensive, particularly when compared to their usefulness. Here is a simplified guide that hopefully will be beneficial to you on your next shopping spree.

Shoes—Rubbersoled, light weight soft shoes are best for dancing jazz as they allow your feet to both breathe and be mobile and prevent you from sticking or slipping on a wood floor. The best type of floors to dance on are wood floors with very little floor treatment. Be extremely cautious of waxed floors. I bring a set of three shoes to every new class I enroll in; one with leather bottoms, one with a very, very fine light rubber sole, and the other with a thick rubber sole. Rubber soles also prevent marking up the wood floors. Check with the studio you are attending as some studio personnel prefer white soles on their floors.

Light weight tennis shoes are also excellent. You can purchase a shoe that resembles a very light weight tennis shoe, but has the advantage of coming in many colors. Most jazz shoes on the market today are extremely expensive and should be purchased only if you are a serious student. They come in canvas and leather, the latter being the most advantageous since the more you wear them, the more they conform to your foot. Purchase a snug fitting pair since they stretch.

Try to avoid heels if at all possible. Heels have the same effect as street shoes with heels; they shorten the achilles and put pressure on the small of your back. Most dancers that are performing in shoes requiring heels will need to practice with them as their "motion center" will be different. If you must wear them, make sure you ankles and legs are in good condition. You should also always stretch your calves. It is essential to perform the standing and floor exercises without shoes so your feet have a full range of motion and good articulation. Many dancers prefer dancing entirely barefoot, although the lack of shoes is limiting on turns. Never dance in full tights without shoes. If your tights are not the stirrup type, try cutting the toes and heels out of your tights. Then you can always put on nylon socks over your feet before putting on your shoes. Avoid wearing socks alone as footwear.

Leg warmers—The purpose of leg warmers is to keep your muscles warm during breaks in dancing since there is a great deal of stop and go motion in a jazz class. However, since there is some controversy on their value, they should be considered optional attire.

Tights—Tights are the coverings over your legs. The best type are the "stretch and sheer" as they have the best "give" and they don't inhibit your dancing. Tights are available in various sizes and colors which are of personal preference. Always try them on and if they fit snugly, purchase the next pair larger. Tights should be laundered in cold water and hung to dry as they tend to lose their elasticity when exposed to high temperatures. You might also want to check with your local dance studio for a possible color code.

Leotard—Leotards for men and women are too numerous to mention in this book. However, I recommend that you try them on as some brand names run their "leos" smaller than marked. Be sure the material breathes—cotton is the best for that. The higher cut legs give the appearance of a longer leg. Some dancers also wear belts as a reminder to lift their stomachs.

Jazz Pants—Jazz pants can also be considered optional dance attire. Again, they should stretch and breathe easily. They are usually worn over tights, but that is a preference. Jazz pants can be purchased with flared or straight legs. The plastic baggie pants on the market today are not recommended. Not only do they inhibit your ability to see your body alignment, but more importantly, they prevent your body from cooling through evaporation. It is not only dangerous to lose large quantities of body fluid, but is almost totally worthless as a weight loss technique because of natural replacement of fluids. Suspenders can be worn with jazz pants and are available in almost any color.

Sweat Shirts—This item is a good investment to avoid a chill after workouts. Refrain from wearing them during class since they greatly reduce anyone's ability to see your body perform.

Hair—A good way to keep your hair away from your face is to purchase a sweatband. Hair in your face can be dangerous as it can blind you while turning.

Jewelry—Of course, all jewelry that might be dangerous to you and other dancers should not be worn.

4 Basic Jazz Positions

The following positions and terms are the most common for jazz dance. Jazz is unique in that it is one of the most natural forms of dancing. Notice that the basic positions of the feet are straight forward and the basic moves are performed "low" to the ground (with bent knees, i.e., in "plié"). Also included are some basic modern and ballet terms frequently used in jazz dance. Become familiar with the following terms as they will be used throughout the book. It is recommended that you assume the position and go through each movement as the description is read.

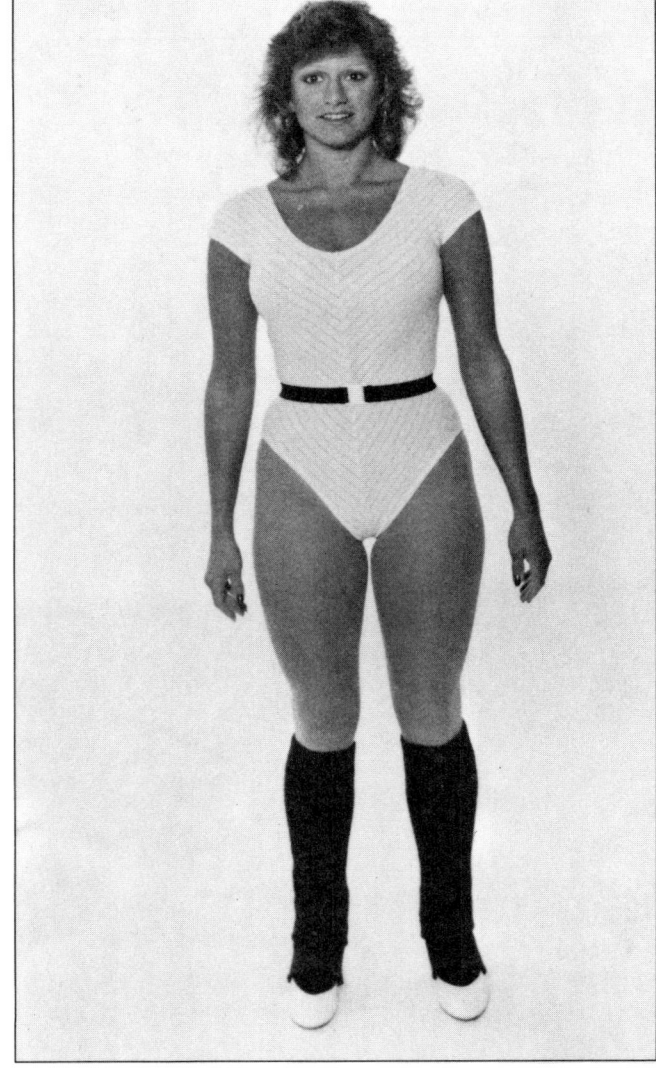

Foot Positions

JAZZ FIRST POSITION—Your feet are parallel, about one to two inches apart with your toes forward.

ALL THAT JAZZ AND MORE... 17

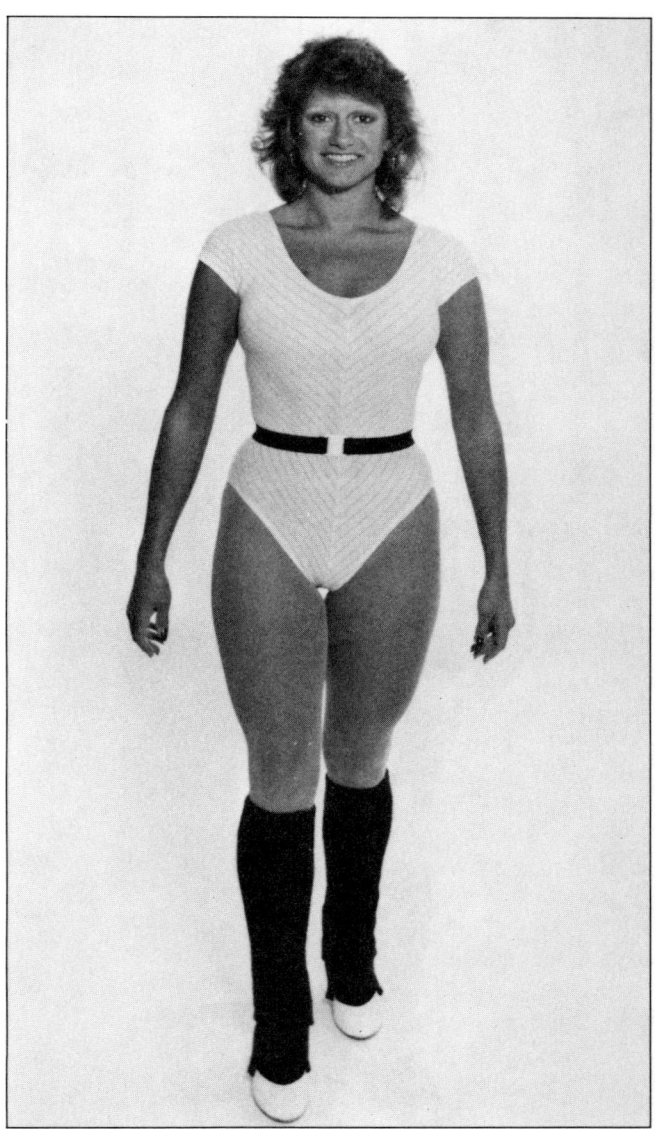

JAZZ FOURTH POSITION—Your feet are separated, approximately twelve inches apart with one foot in front of the other with your toes forward.

JAZZ SECOND POSITION—Your feet are parallel, approximately shoulder width apart with your toes forward.

18 BASIC JAZZ POSITIONS

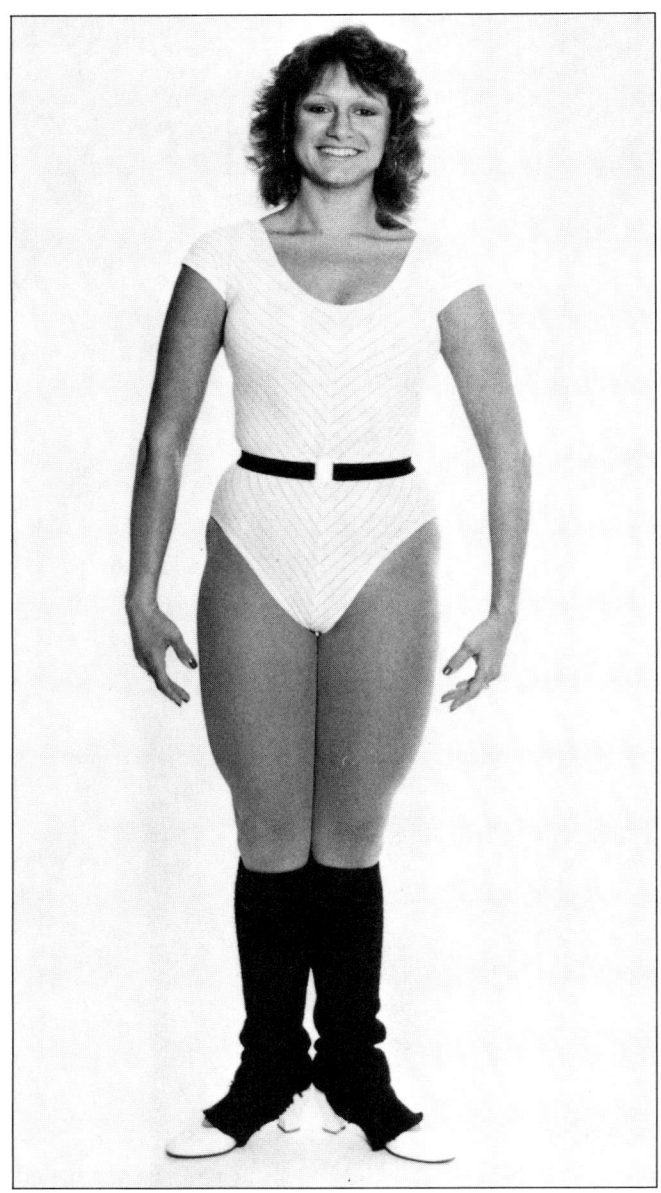

BALLET FIRST POSITION—Your heels are together and your legs rotated outward from your hips. Note: Do not force a 180° turn-out. Only turn-out to a point where it feels comfortable and secure and can be maintained without disturbing your body alignment.

BALLET SECOND POSITION—Your legs are turned out from your hips; your heels are approximately twelve inches apart.

ALL THAT JAZZ AND MORE... 19

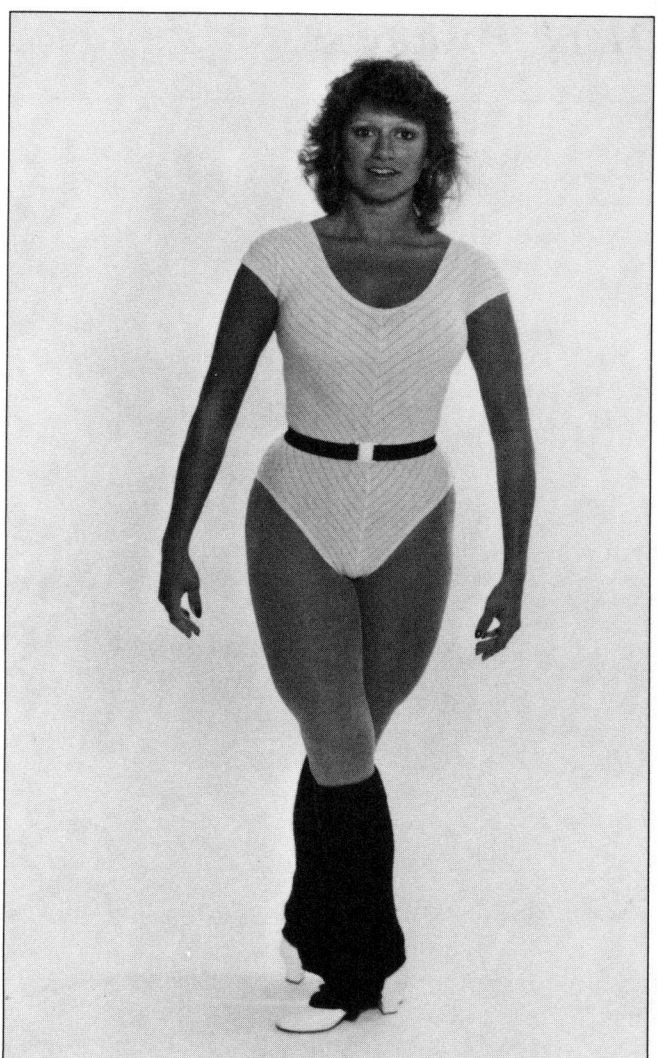

BALLET FIFTH POSITION—Same as ballet fourth position, only with the heel of your front foot placed at the joint of the toes of your back foot.

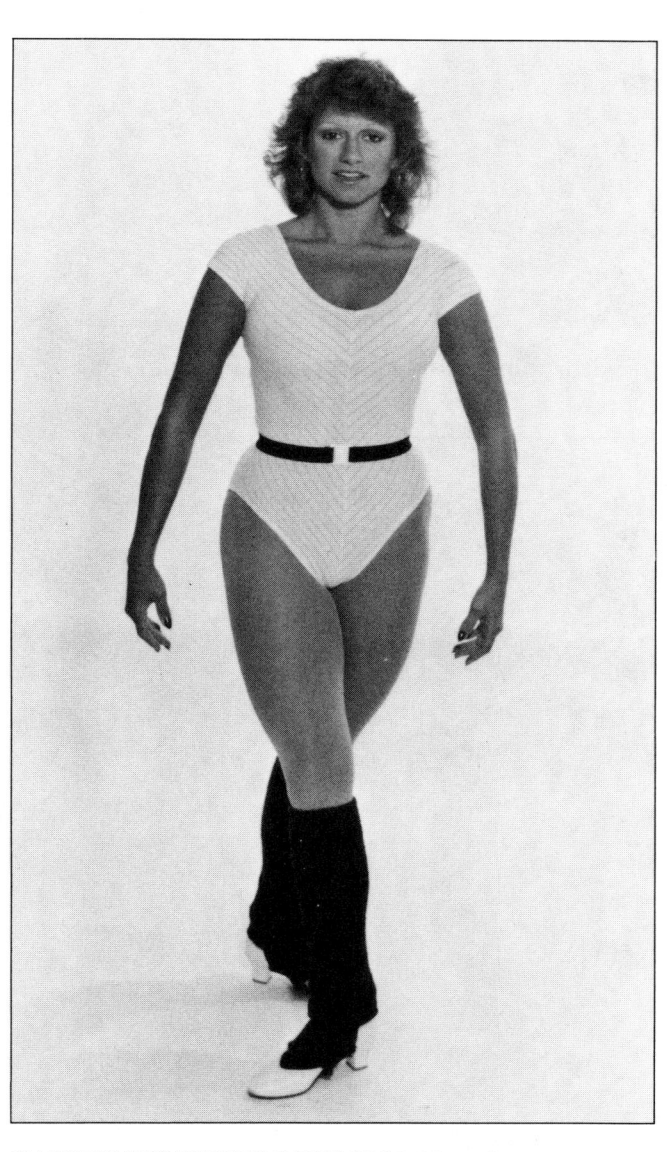

BALLET FOURTH POSITION—Your legs are turned out from your hips with one foot approximately one foot directly in front of the other.

Hand Positions

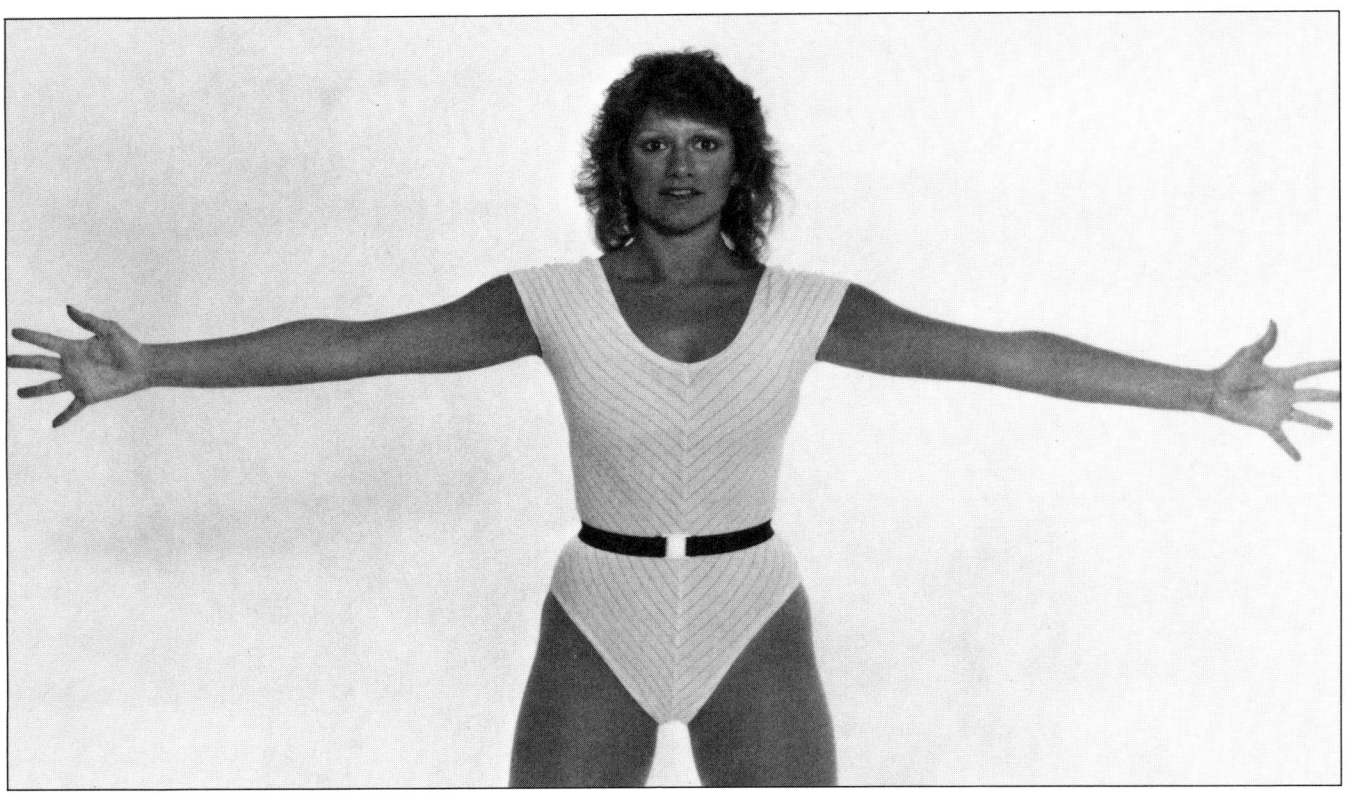

JAZZ PALMS—Your fingers are spread and fully extended with your hands in a plane surface.

JAZZ HANDS—Your palms face downward with your fingers and hands in a relaxed position.

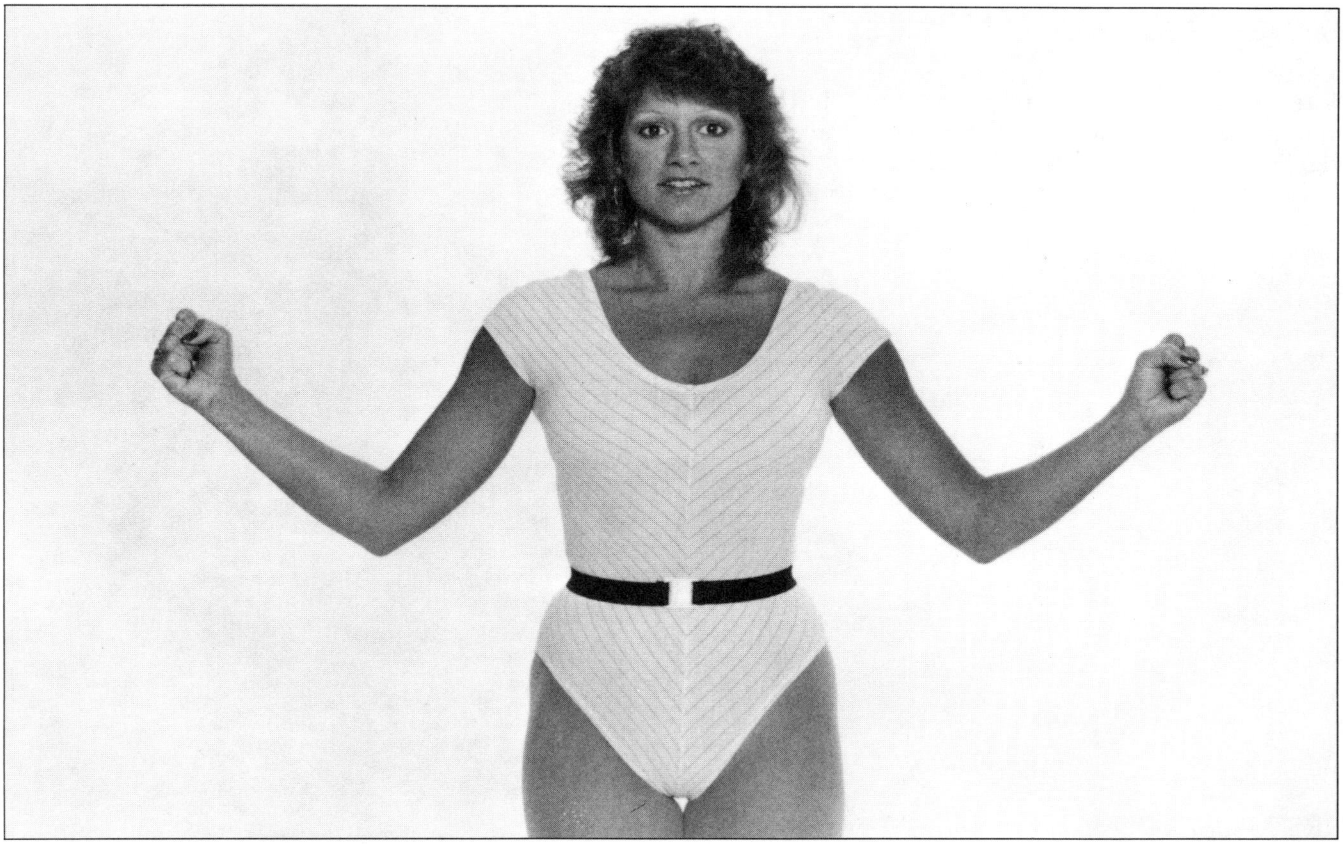

ALL THAT JAZZ AND MORE... 21

JAZZ FISTS—Illustrated with bent arms.

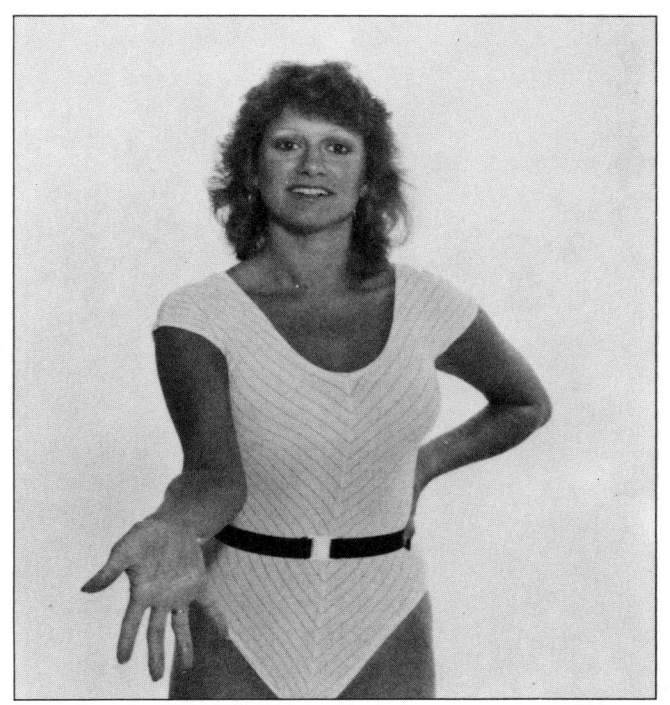

JAZZ WRIST FAN—Your hands rotate inward or outward with your fingers spread and your wrists bent.

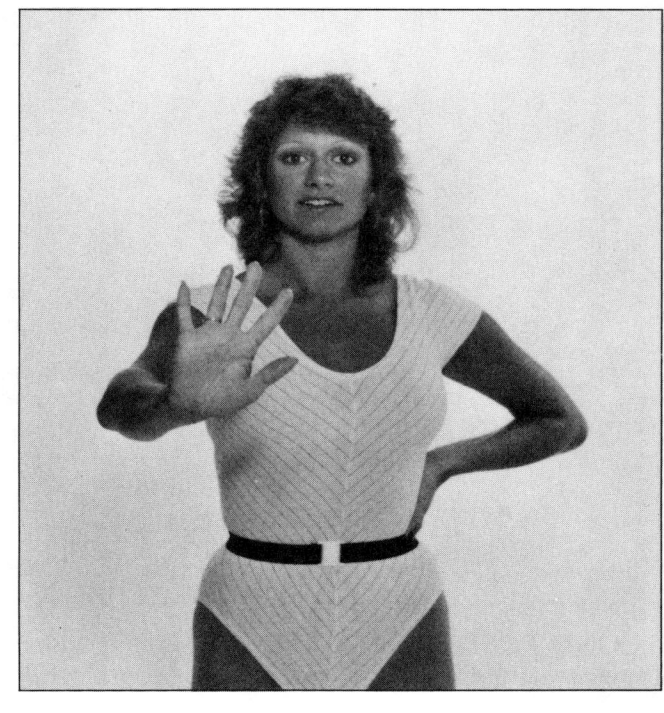

Arm Positions

Note: All arm positions are done slightly in front of your body. If you were to look straight ahead and wiggle your fingers in any of the given positions, you should see them out of your peripheral vision.

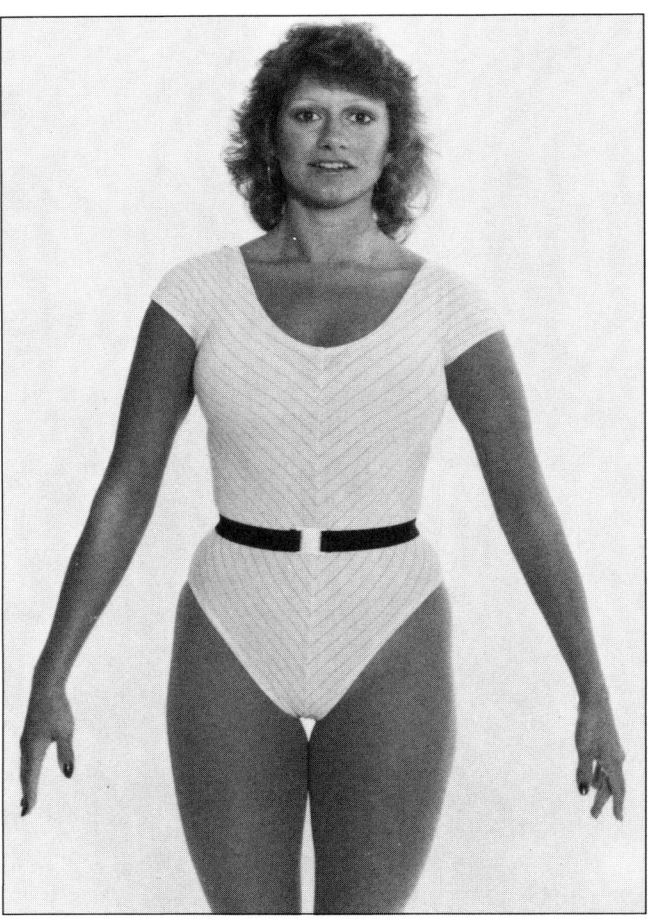

FIRST POSITION JAZZ ARMS—Your elbows are straight with your arms down and slightly outward from body. Turn your palms inward.

SECOND POSITION LONG JAZZ ARMS—Your elbows are lifted and your arms held horizontal with your palms down and your arms slightly in front of your shoulders.

THIRD POSITION JAZZ ARMS—One arm may be extended forward at rib cage level with your palm down or placed high with your other arm in a jazz second position.

24 BASIC JAZZ POSITIONS

FOURTH POSITION JAZZ ARMS—Either arm may be high. The raised arm has an outward palm and your other arm is at the fork of your ribs with its palm facing downward.

HIGH FIFTH POSITION JAZZ ARMS—Your arms are overhead but angled slightly outward from your body with your palms inward or outward.

DIAGONAL JAZZ ARMS—One arm overhead and slightly outward with your palm out. Place your other arm down and slightly outward with your palm in. Your arms should form a straight line.

JAZZ PRESS—Your arms press outward to the second position with your wrist hyperflexed and your palms outward.

26 BASIC JAZZ POSITIONS

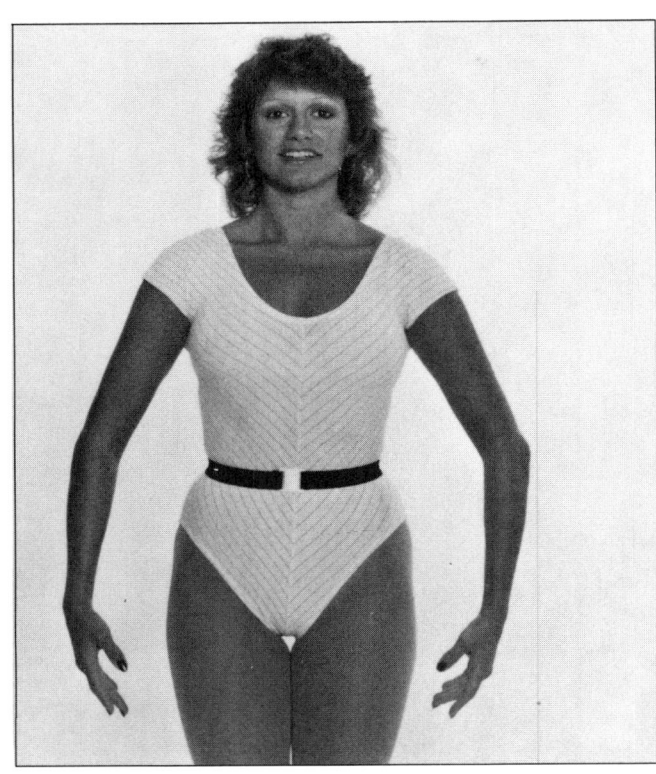

FIRST POSITION BALLET ARMS—Your arms are slightly curved and downward. Your palms face your body and your fingertips just touch the sides of your thighs.

SECOND POSITION BALLET ARMS—Your arms are open to your side with a slight curve downward with ¾ of each palm held open to the front. (Imagine yourself hugging a huge redwood tree!)

ALL THAT JAZZ AND MORE... 27

en avant

en haut

THIRD POSITION BALLET ARMS—Either arm may be in front. The hand of the front arm is centered on your body, thus forming a half-circle in each of the positions; the other arm is in the second position.

28 BASIC JAZZ POSITIONS

FOURTH POSITION BALLET ARMS—Either arm may be high. The raised arm forms a half-circle above your head; the other arm forms a half-circle opposite the fork in your ribs.

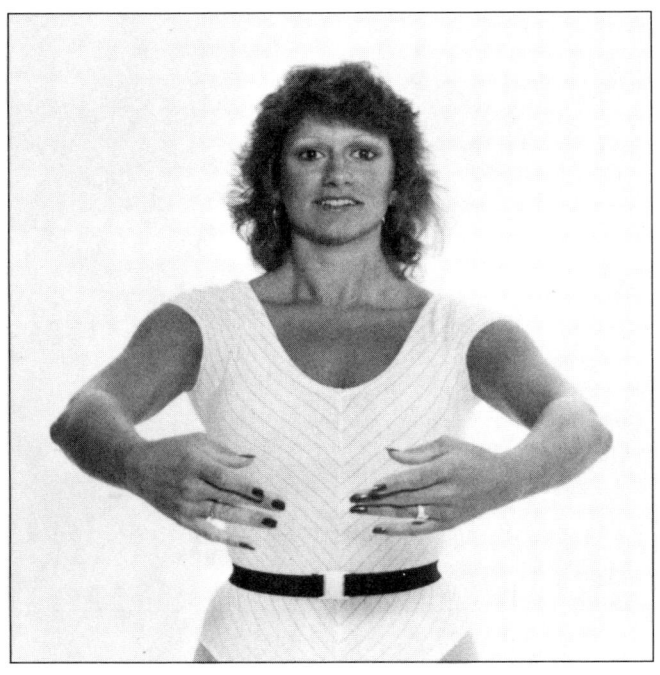

en avant

en haut

FIFTH POSITION BALLET ARMS—Your arms form a circle in front of or overhead your body with your hands only a few inches apart and your palms facing each other.

OTHER TERMS AND POSITIONS

PLIÉ (ple a)—A position or a movement referring to lowering the level of your body by bending your knees. On a demi-plié your heels do not rise off the floor as you lower. Instead press your heels into the floor, which will cause your achilles tendon to stretch. A grand plié occurs after a demi-plié position and allows your heels to lift, except in second position where your heels remain on the floor.

Demi-plié

Grand plié

30   BASIC JAZZ POSITIONS

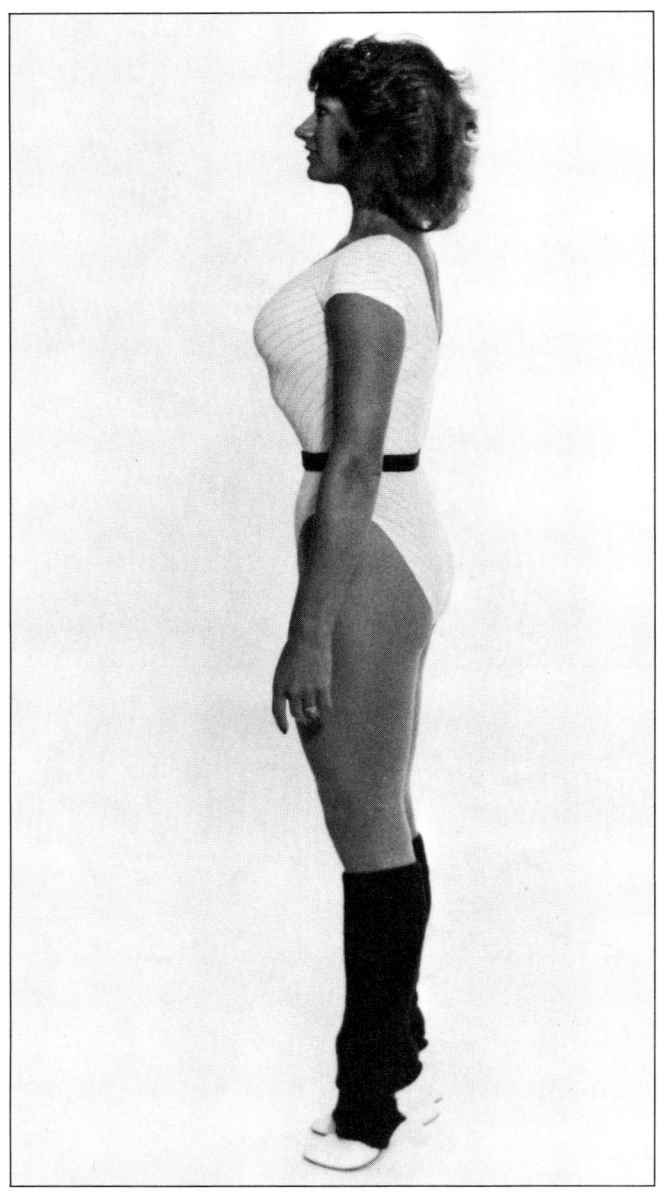

RELEVÉ (reh leh vay)—Rise to the ball of your foot (or both feet). This is also called planter flexion.

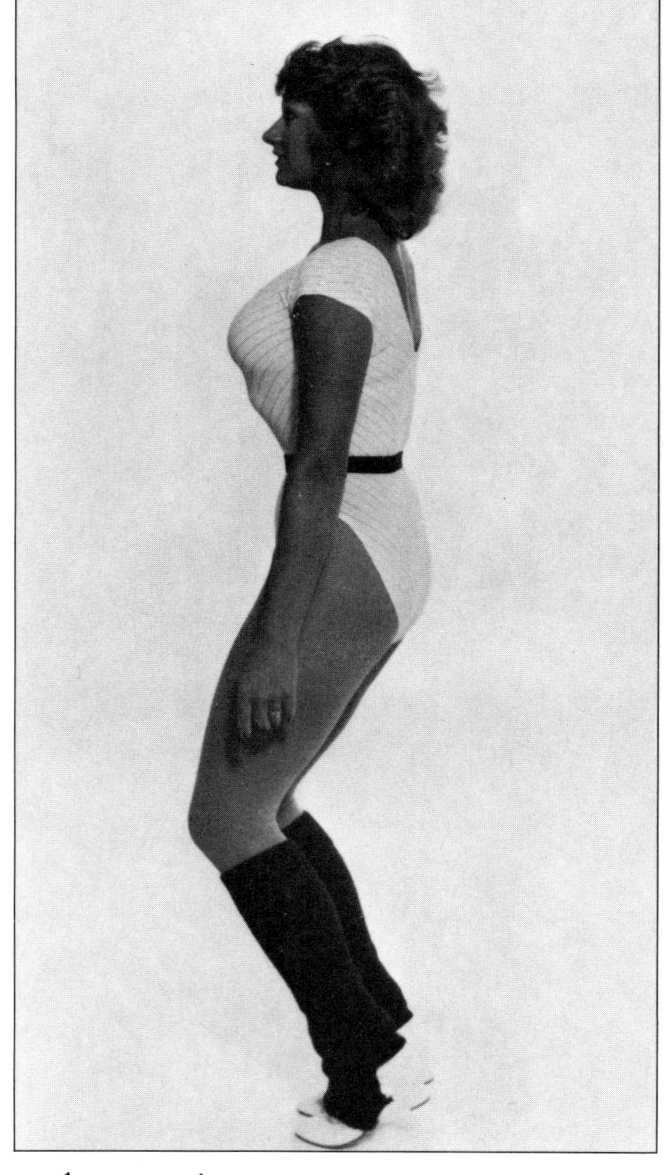

PLIÉ—RELEVÉ POSITION—Standard combination position used quite often in jazz.

ALL THAT JAZZ AND MORE... 31

Outward

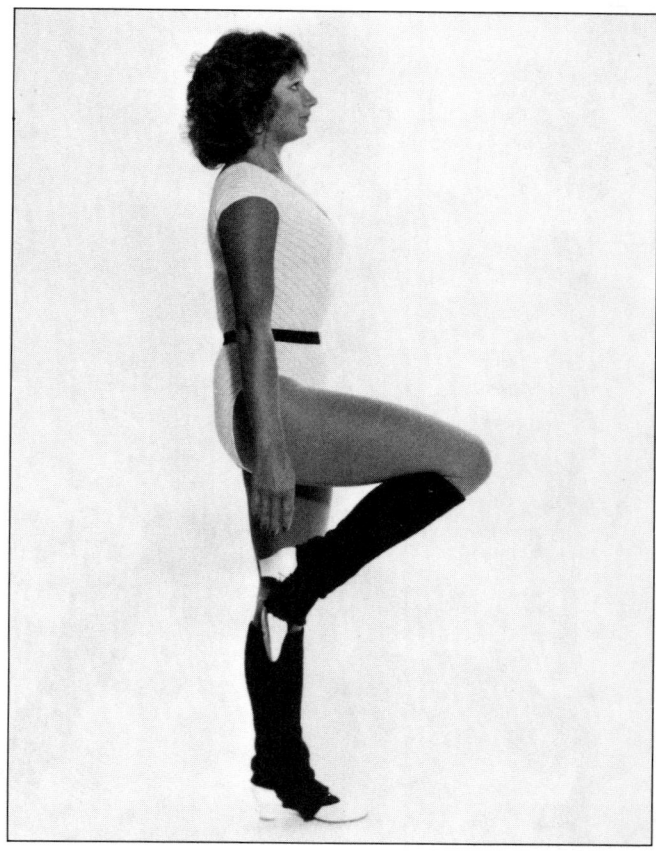

Forward

Inward

PASSÉ (pah say)—Bent knee lifted, toes to opposite knee. The toes of your free leg touch the inside of your supporting knee. An inward passé can also be done with your knees together as one foot is lifted and extended to the side. (The foot position varies on an outward passé from the lower calf to the knee).

32 BASIC JAZZ POSITIONS

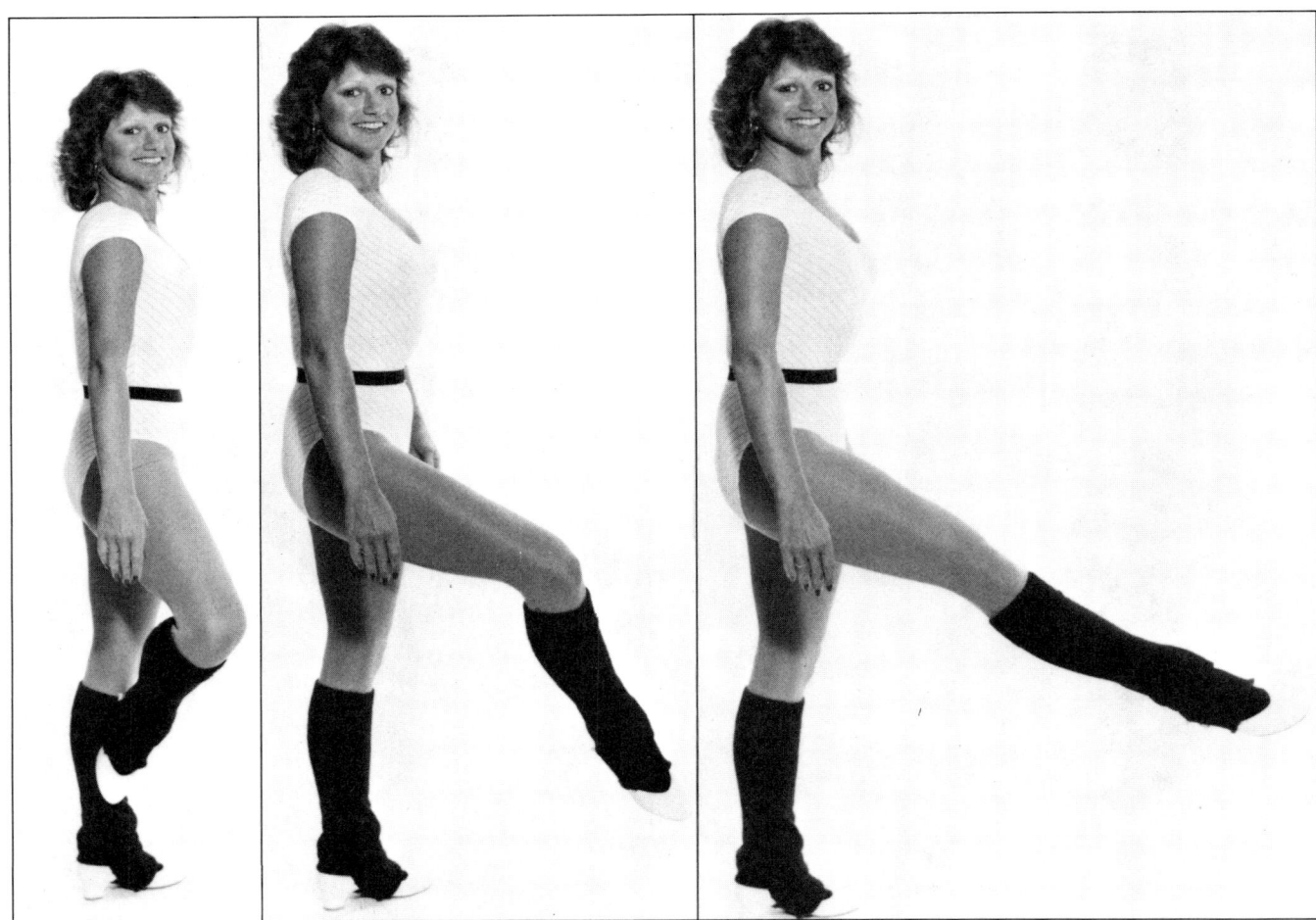

DÉVELOPPÉ (deh-veh-loh-pay)—Your leg is "developed" from a bent knee position to an open position or a straight leg position.

ALL THAT JAZZ AND MORE... 33

Turned Out

Forward

Turned In

LUNGE FORWARD—With either leg straight, your other leg is bent after a forward stepping motion.

34 BASIC JAZZ POSITIONS

Turned Out

Forward

Turned In

LUNGE SIDE—Same as before only performed in second position.

LUNGE WITH HIP LIFT—Your hip is lifted prior to assuming a lunge position.

HINGE—Lean backward with a straight back in plié-relevé position.

BODY ARCH—Curve your entire body in a given direction.

Side

Back

36 BASIC JAZZ POSITIONS

CONTRACTION—An upper body contraction occurs as you contract your abdominal or stomach muscles; lower body contraction is a tilting of your pelvic area backwards.

BODY ROLL—A body roll occurs from your feet up beginning in a demi-plié position. Roll your knees forward first, then your hips, chest, arms and head.

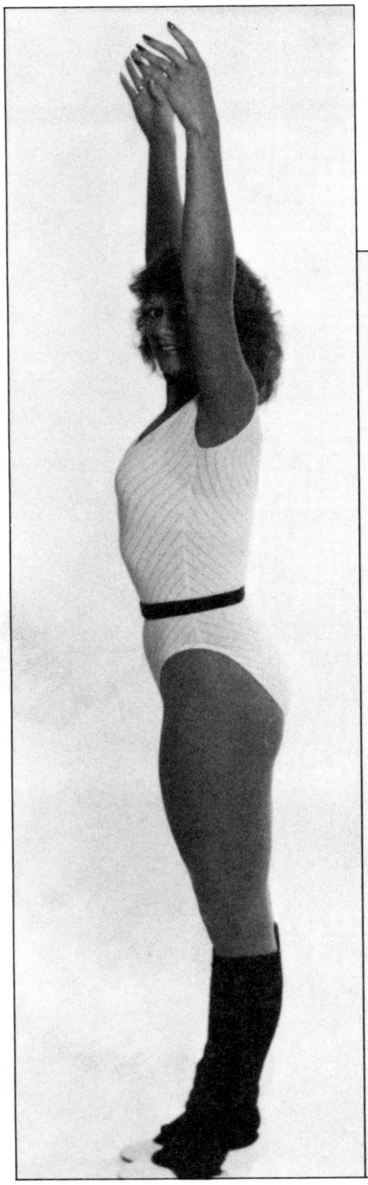

ALL THAT JAZZ AND MORE... 37

ARABESQUE (air ă běsk)—Your body is balanced over one foot with your other leg fully extended either on the ground or lifted. Your arms can be in a variety of positions.

DRAG—Slide your second foot toward your weight bearing lead foot.

38 BASIC JAZZ POSITIONS

ATTITUDE—A pose on one leg with your other leg lifted and bent at the knee. The knee of your lifted leg should be at a same or higher level than the foot.

JAZZ SPLIT—Your back leg is bent and your front leg is straight in a hurdle sitting position. *See Page 174*

SPLITS—Your front knee faces the ceiling and your back leg is turned out (knee facing slightly out). *See page 71*

SWASTIKA (swă stĭk ă)—Both knees are bent under your body; arm position optional. *See page 15*

5 Center Floor Exercise Technique

Good posture and alignment are extremely beneficial and necessary in jazz dance. Otherwise, you may not be strengthening or stretching the desired muscles or you may be limiting yourself in executing dance movements. Most importantly, you may be susceptible to injury, especially in the back region. Thus, for balance, for safety, for turns, and for control, good posture is essential.

For good posture, some thoughts to remember are to:

- Imagine yourself in between two sheets of glass.
- Hold your spine straight by lengthening your vertebrae.
- Keep your neck free from tension by relaxing your shoulders.
- Lift your rib cage up and in.
- Lift your stomach by feeling your stomach muscles both pulling toward your back and lifting directly under your rib cage.
- Your pelvis should be straight, neither dropped forward nor tucked under. When your pelvis is incorrectly tilted forward, the weight of your upper body is carried in front of the legs—an alignment which can cause lower back strain. Because of the stress an incorrect alignment places on your back, you should be particularly careful to ensure that you assume the proper position at all times.

When your body is correctly held and balanced, it is called your body's "center" in dance. You will always be reaching for your center throughout your dancing, as it is a source of control, especially in turning. Stop...close your eyes and feel this position. Now with your eyes closed, visualize your upper body continuing to grow while at the same time imagine "pressing" into the ground. This lengthening process will teach you the lift and stretch that is so important in dance.

As you perform the following exercises, mentally reach beyond your physical capabilities—always stretching. Try to become aware of every part of your body. Feel and look alert. Your body can express energy just by the way you hold yourself. And lastly, enjoy!

Each exercise is performed to eight counts. Once the eight count rhythm is accomplished, the counts can be reduced and quickened. Remember, do all exercises at Level I and then progress through the levels as you advance.

R = Right   L = Left   AST = At the Same Time

Overall Body Stretch

Level I—Begin in a ballet second position; cross L behind R pressing your heel into the ground; your arms cross at your wrists above your head; repeat other side.

ALL THAT JAZZ AND MORE... 41

Level I—Begin in a jazz second position; reach for the sky, alternating your arms and concentrating on placement. Feel the size of your body stretch as you plié-relevé the same side you are stretching.

Level I—In Jazz second position; open your arms to second position while concentrating on breathing; AST arch your upper body and release your head and back.

Level I—Jazz second position; reach forward with a flat back; your weight is forward on your toes; your stomach is lifted; your head is in a neutral position.

Fold your upper body over and relax; imagine the small of your back reaching for your knees to give the best stretch. Contract back and slowly roll your body up to a standing position, concentrating on the proper placement of your spine.

Note: Believe it or not, this exercise has created some recent controversy and may place undue stress on one of the main supporting ligaments of the spine and sciatic nerve. Therefore, use with caution.

44 CENTER FLOOR EXERCISE TECHNIQUE

Level II—With your feet together and parallel, roll your body with clasped hands behind your back for upper back stretch. Maintain a flat back as you flex your body and drop your head towards the floor.

ALL THAT JAZZ AND MORE... 45

Level I—Slow, controlled trunk circles with your arms circling overhead, keeping your pelvis in alignment.

Level I—Jazz second position; controlled side stretches to L, leading with your rib cage. Rotate to a flat back position and fold over toward one foot. Reach out to the side again and circle your trunk to the R side. Rotate your hips under as your trunk rotates to the side. Stretch to an upright position; repeat other side.

Level II—Ballet second position; demi-plié R knee with your arms in a high fifth position. Swing your torso through to a second position; stretch by bending your trunk first to the R side, then forward, then to the other side; bend L knee as R straightens; return and repeat other side.

Level II—Ballet second position; bend R knee; lift your heel; slowly side stretch to L. Slowly return trunk; contract the small of your back, AST bring R knee in; plié R as far as possible in plie-relevé position; straighten your knee; return to the second position; repeat other side.

ALL THAT JAZZ AND MORE... **47**

Leg Stretching and Strengthening

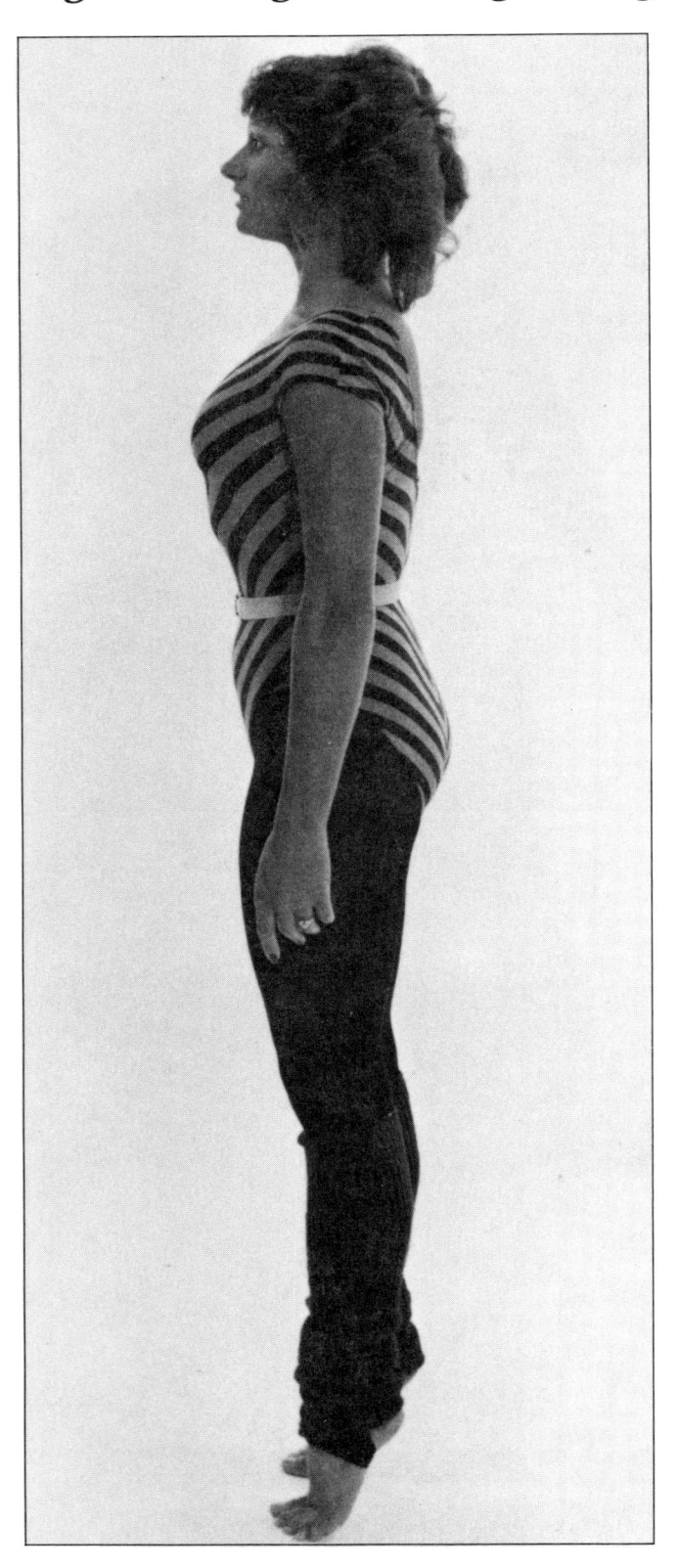

Level I—Jazz first position; rise up and down on your toes three times; hold the last time for eight counts in relevé position; keep your heels together and your weight centered on the balls of your feet.

Level III—Same as Level I, only rise up and down on the toes of one foot only.

Level II—From ballet fourth position, demi-plié; come up to sous-sus (pronounced sue-sue) position (feet close tightly in fifth position on relevé); repeat from second position; fourth position in back and second position again; reverse feet.

50 CENTER FLOOR EXERCISE TECHNIQUE

Level I—Demi-plié in jazz first position twice; then grand plié. Repeat in ballet first, second, fourth, and fifth positions.

Level II—Demi-plié in jazz first position; lift your heels keeping your knees bent; straighten your legs and lower your heels, then relevé; demi-plié with your heels still lifted; place your heels down and straighten your legs. Repeat in ballet first, second, fourth, and fifth positions. (See note on pliés at end of this section.)

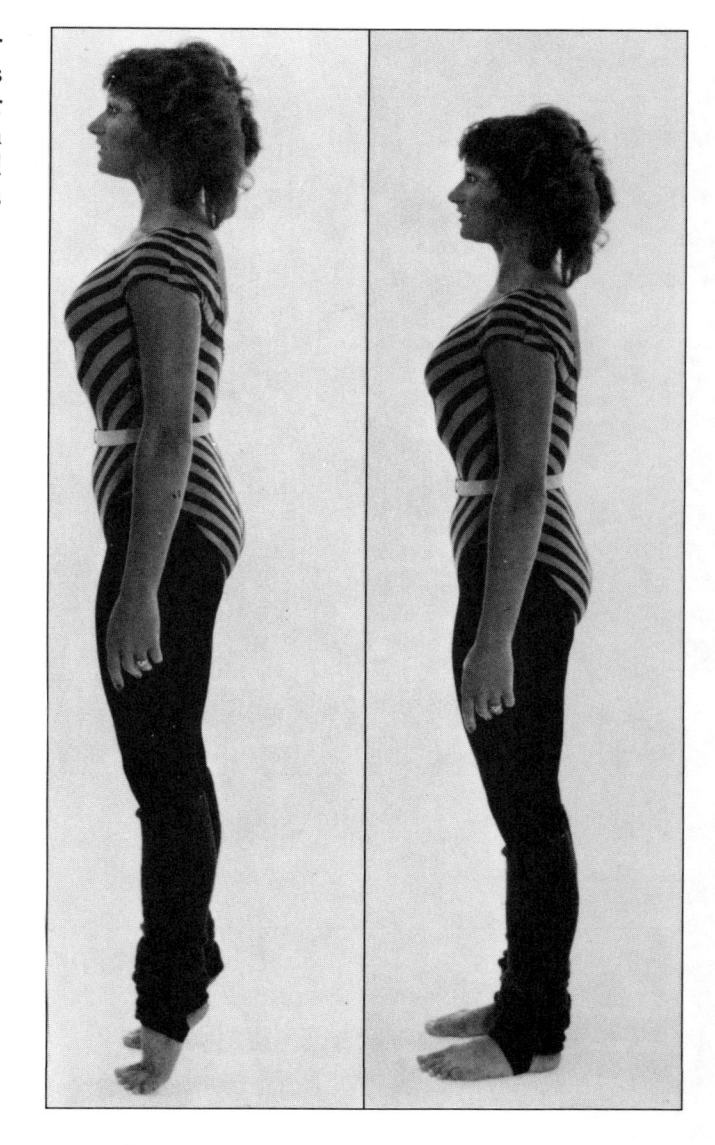

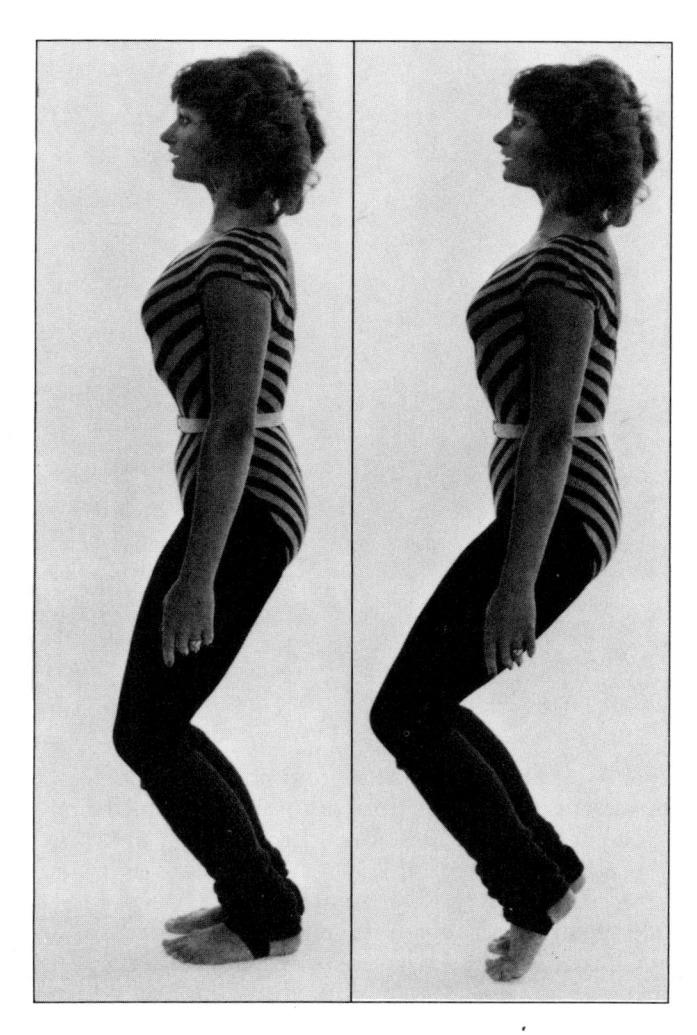

Level I—Grand plié in the second position, with your arms in the second position; pivot 90° to L side bringing R knee in; R arm swings through first and port de bras (carriage of the arms) backward with an arched body; stretch forward into a deep lunge making sure your weight is centered, not forward or backward; straighten your leg, trying to keep your chest on your knee; reach your trunk out and return.

ALL THAT JAZZ AND MORE... 53

54 CENTER FLOOR EXERCISE TECHNIQUE

Level II—Repeat as before, only flex your foot when straightening your leg in the lunge position.

Level III—Same as Level II, only rotate your hips side to side in the lunge position.

Note: If done correctly, pliés can stretch some of the muscles of your thighs, such as the adductors, and can strengthen some muscles, such as the hamstrings and quadriceps. Skeletal joint range is probably increased through their use. If pliés are performed incorrectly (i.e., pelvis forward), they will probably do more damage than good.

56 CENTER FLOOR EXERCISE TECHNIQUE

Exercise Technique for Jumps

Level I—In order to prepare for jumps, your feet and legs must be warmed up properly. In a jazz first position point your foot forward with the ball of your foot, then your toes. Press your foot into the ground to lift your thigh. Return to first position. Do the same from a ballet first position, pointing to the side; repeat other side.

ALL THAT JAZZ AND MORE... 57

Level I—Jazz first position; eight small jumps in place making sure you land in demi-plié after each jump.

Level II—Jazz first position; perform eight tuck jumps keeping your chest lifted and bringing your knees to your chest.

Level I—Eight small jumps from ballet first, second, and fifth position, reversing your feet in the fifth position after each jump.

Level II—Eight straddle jumps from jazz first position, starting low and gradually getting wider and wider.

6
Floor Exercise Technique

If preferred, the floor technique series can precede the center technique series. Some instructors believe nothing should be attempted standing unless it first can be done sitting. Others feel the need to demonstrate and exercise the upper body while on the floor before demonstrating in a standing position. I feel your entire body should be warmed up before isolating separate muscle groups.

All the techniques illustrated in this section should be performed in a slow and sustained manner. Show complete control coming into and going out of the exercises. The primary purpose of the stretching exercises are to warm up your muscles, not specifically to increase flexibility. Stretching exercises need to be held thirty to sixty seconds in order to increase flexibility. Logically, stretching should be done directly after class on the dancer's own time and while the tissue temperature is still high. (See S-T-R-E-T-C-H-ability Chapter.)

Over three-fourths of the United States' population suffers from lower back problems sometime in their life. That's a very large and significant percentage. During the floor series, the majority of attention will be focused on lower back placement. Our first exercise will increase awareness in that area.

Pelvic Tilt

Level I—Lie in a supine position; keep your knees up and your arms out to the side. Press the small of your back into the floor; hold for eight counts, continuing to breathe normally; relax; repeat eight times.

60 *FLOOR EXERCISE TECHNIQUE*

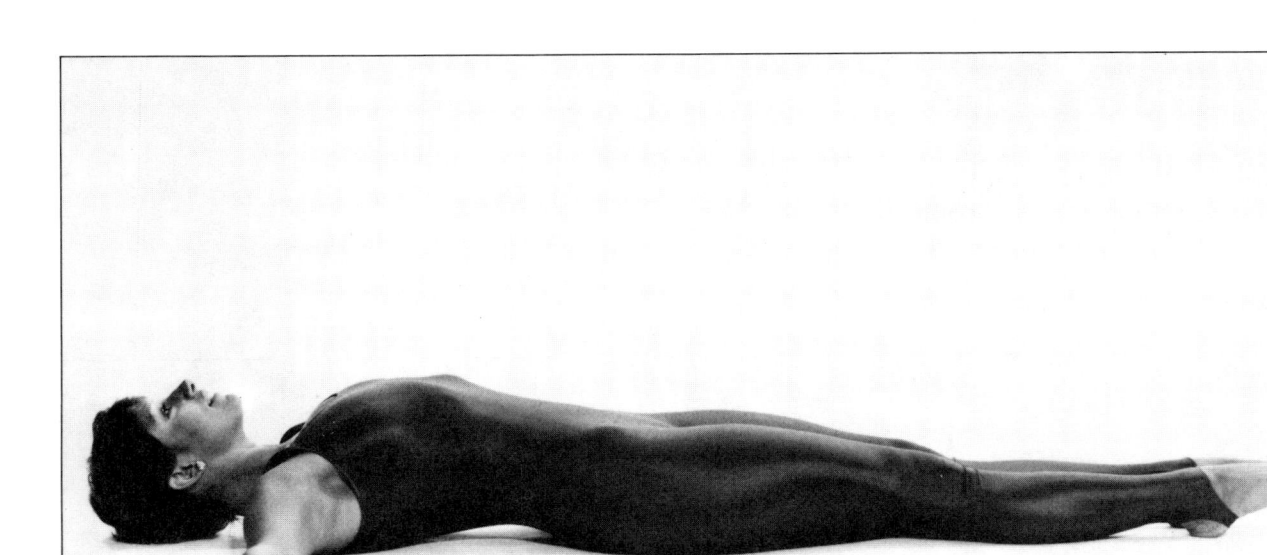

Level II—Do as before only with straight legs.

Abdominal Strength

Level I—Your stomach muscles are your best protector for proper pelvic alignment. Weak abdominal muscles can cause forward pelvic tilt. Lie in a supine position with your knees bent; place your hands on your knees and curl your trunk up until your fingertips touch the top of your knees. Roll down slowly, taking eight counts. Repeat at least ten times.

Level II—Repeat Level I twenty times.
Level III—Repeat Level I at least forty times.
Note: You have muscles in your stomach that crisscross. You can increase the effectiveness of your exercise and strengthen these muscles by performing these curls with a rotation at the completion (example: R hand on L knee).

62 FLOOR EXERCISE TECHNIQUE

Level III—From a supine position, maintain a flat pelvic position and bring your knees to your chest for four counts; straighten your legs to a vertical position for four counts and lower your legs to the floor for eight counts. Repeat at least ten times. Variation: try a turn-out position at the same time alternate crossing your legs slightly while lowering.

Abdominal Stretch

Level I—In order to avoid muscle cramping at the beginning level, always stretch a muscle after a strengthening exercise. In a supine position; knees bent with your feet flat on the floor; your arms to the side; lift your pelvis by tilting your pelvis backward for eight counts. Hold that position for eight counts, then slowly lower yourself by rolling your back onto the ground, feeling each vertebrae.

Level II—Same as before, only instead of holding the lifted position, alternate lifting your hips for four counts each; reduce to two counts; then to one count.

Level III—Same exercise as Level I before, only extend one leg in the air as you lift your pelvis and hold.

Groin Stretch and Control

Level I—This is a good stretch to prepare for side kicks and second position splits. In a supine position with the soles of your feet together and flat on the floor with your knees bent; your hands clasped overhead. Bring your hands to your chest and curl up to a flat back position. Continue forward with a flat back as long as possible; round over grasping your ankles; "scoop" your back into a flat back position with your shoulders down; then roll back to the floor and bring your arms overhead.

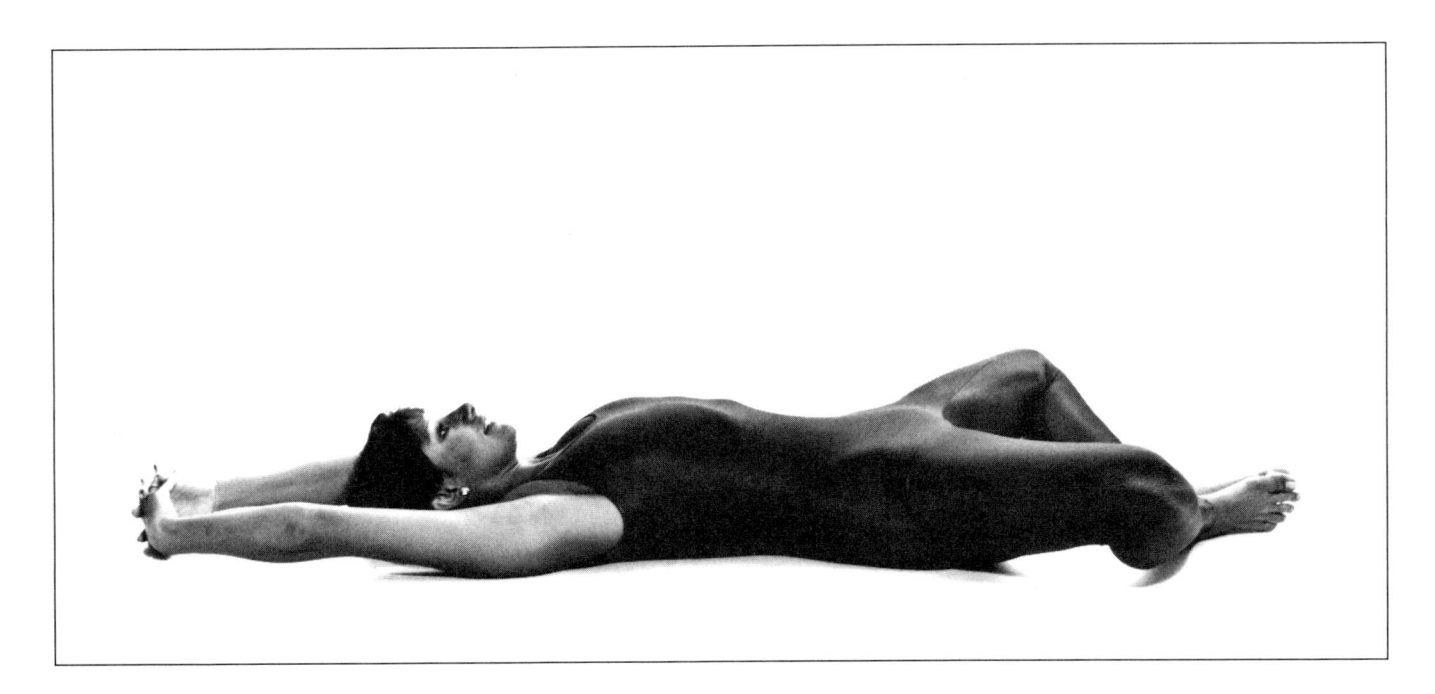

ALL THAT JAZZ AND MORE... 65

Level II—Same beginning position as Level I; bring your arms to your chest and come up to a sitting position. Your arms then come down and R arm grabs R foot; straighten your leg keeping your back upright. Cross your chest with your leg, stretching your outside leg muscles; bring your leg to a second position, stretching the inside of your leg in the upright position; repeat other side.

Back and Leg Stretch and Control

Level I—In a supine position with straight legs, bring your knees to your chest; slowly and cautiously straighten and extend legs upward (do not force). Keep your spine flat on the ground; flex your feet with your heels reaching toward the sky; planter flex your ankles; then point your toes; bend your knees again. Roll back with your knees trying to touch the floor by your ears; hold; return and repeat.

68   FLOOR EXERCISE TECHNIQUE

Level II—Same as Level I only reach your knees to the floor beside your ears when extending your legs overhead, straighten your legs and hold. (See note below).

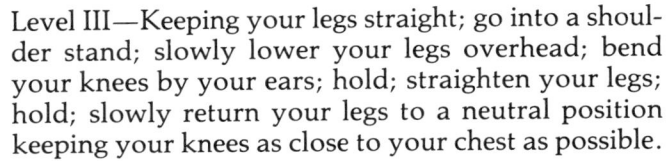

Level III—Keeping your legs straight; go into a shoulder stand; slowly lower your legs overhead; bend your knees by your ears; hold; straighten your legs; hold; slowly return your legs to a neutral position keeping your knees as close to your chest as possible.

Note: When your feet are overhead, this exercise is also known as the yoga plow. Those who lack leg and back flexibility or who have had no previous dance or gymnastics background should avoid this stretch.

Inner Leg Stretch and Control

Level I—In a supine position with legs extended upward, rotate your hips outward pressing the back of your legs together; flex your feet for a calf stretch; point your feet and split your legs to a second position, keeping the small of your back and buttocks on the floor. Rotate your feet outward about the ankle joint in a circle eight times; rotate inward; plié inward keeping your knees lower to the floor than your ankles; développé outward; repeat twice, gradually increasing your speed. Using resistance, imagine someone "pressing" against your legs as they return together to an upright position.

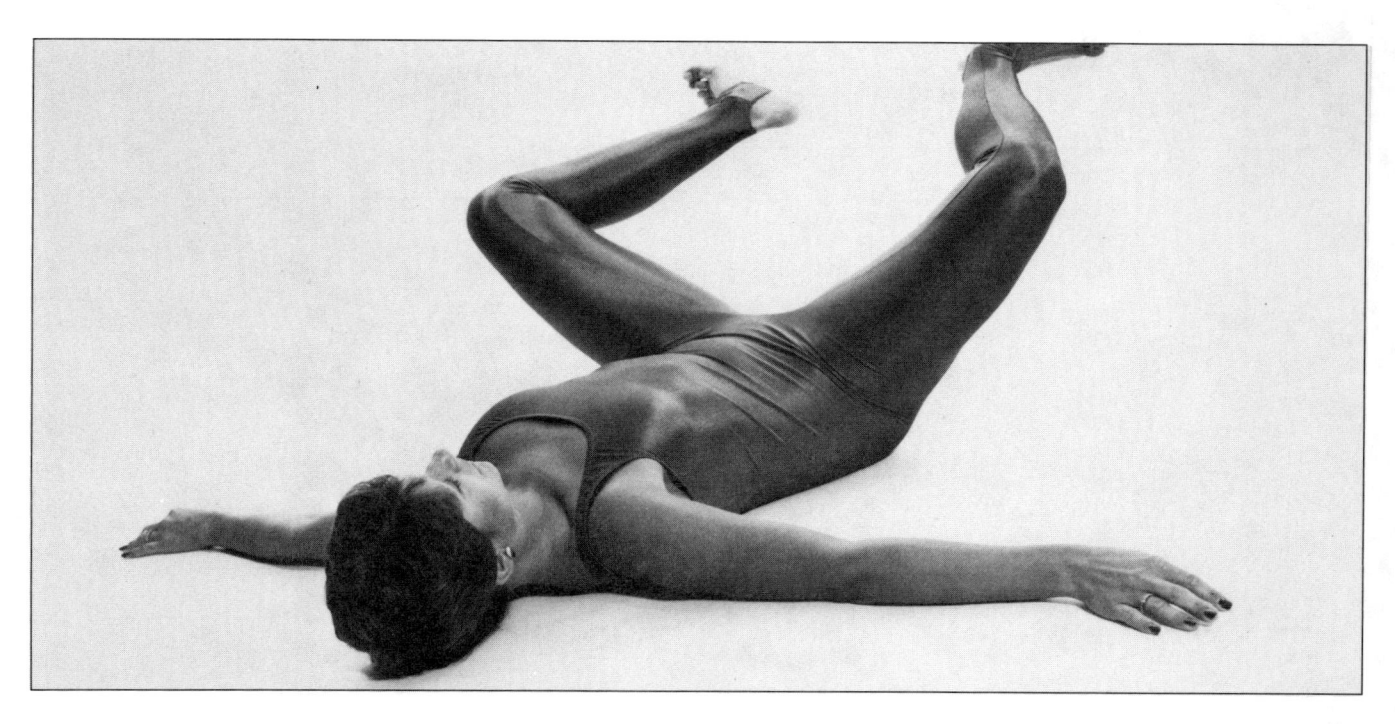

Leg Stretch for Splits and Kicks

Level I—In a supine position, using your arms bring R knee to your chest; your body from the base of your skull to the bottom of your spine should remain in contact with the floor; développé R leg holding onto your ankle if possible; hold four counts. Your leg crosses your body while keeping your hips on the floor; hold; your leg crosses again to the second position while trying to touch your ear with your foot. Do not lose your body alignment; hold for four counts; slowly return your leg to the beginning position; repeat other side.

ALL THAT JAZZ AND MORE... 71

Level II—Your foot is in the second position; roll into a side splits position keeping chest to your knee; hold; roll back and return your leg; repeat other side.

Level III—Repeat as before, when in a splits position, arch your back without using your hands; then bend your back knee; (avoid bending knee if you suffer any previous knee trouble) grab your ankle with your hand and stretch your thigh.

Hip and Turn-Out Stretch

Level I—In a supine position, cross R knee to L shoulder with your knee bent; hold; bring R ankle to L knee; rotate your hip outward and turn your knee out; hold; repeat other side.

Back Strength and Stretch

Level I—In a supine position with your hands at your side; lift your chest upward by arching your back and tilting your pelvis forward. Use your hands to assist by pressing down on the floor; return trunk by pressing the small of your back into the floor first; then contract your pelvis and roll each vertebrae slowly into the ground.

Level II—Try to accomplish the above movement with your arms in the second position but without the support or use of your hands.

Level III—Same exercise, only cross your arms over your chest.

Note: Any backward arches of the spine are unnatural and should only be attempted by those who do not have back problems.

74 FLOOR EXERCISE TECHNIQUE

Level III—In the supine position, lift your chest as before and immediately rise to a pike position stretch; hold. Roll up to a flat back position; contract your abdominals (rear pelvic tilt); AST open your palms; then roll down slowly to a supine position keeping your chin to your chest.

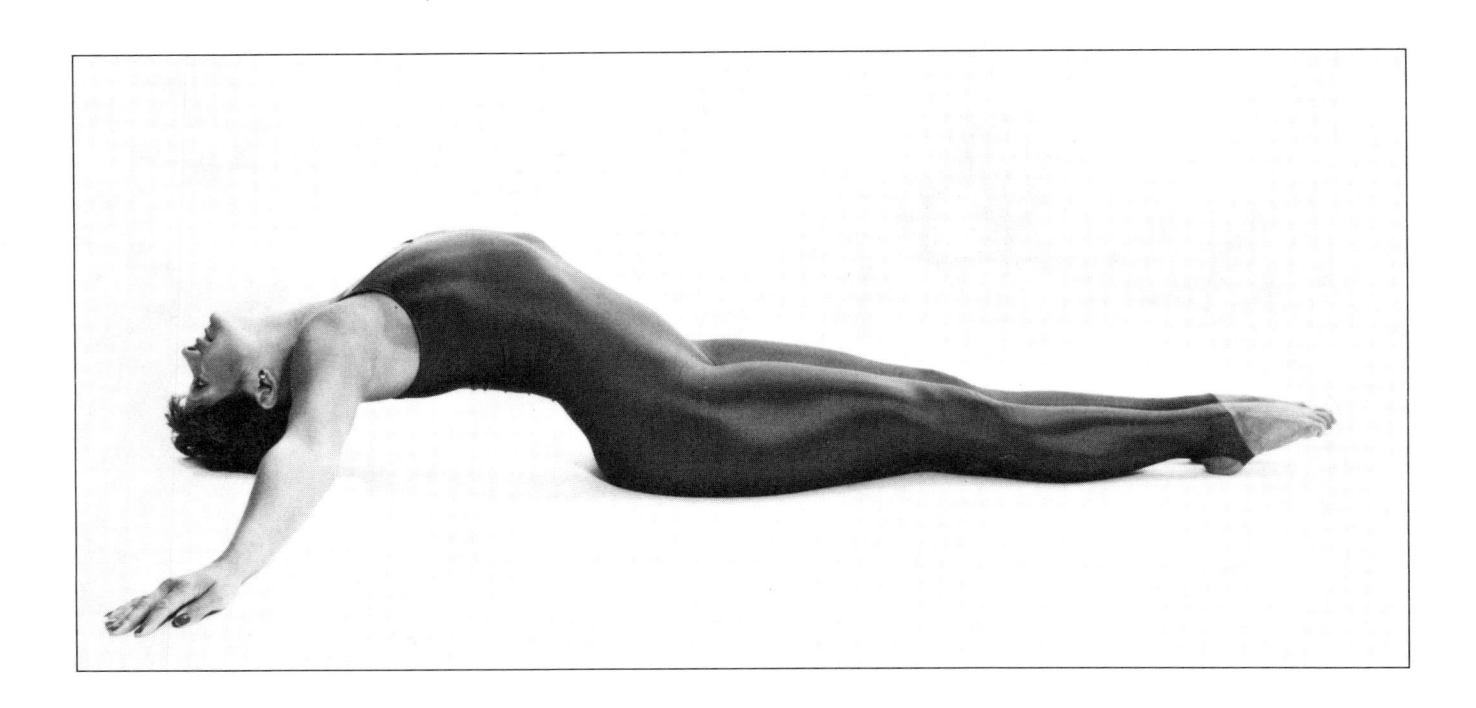

ALL THAT JAZZ AND MORE... 75

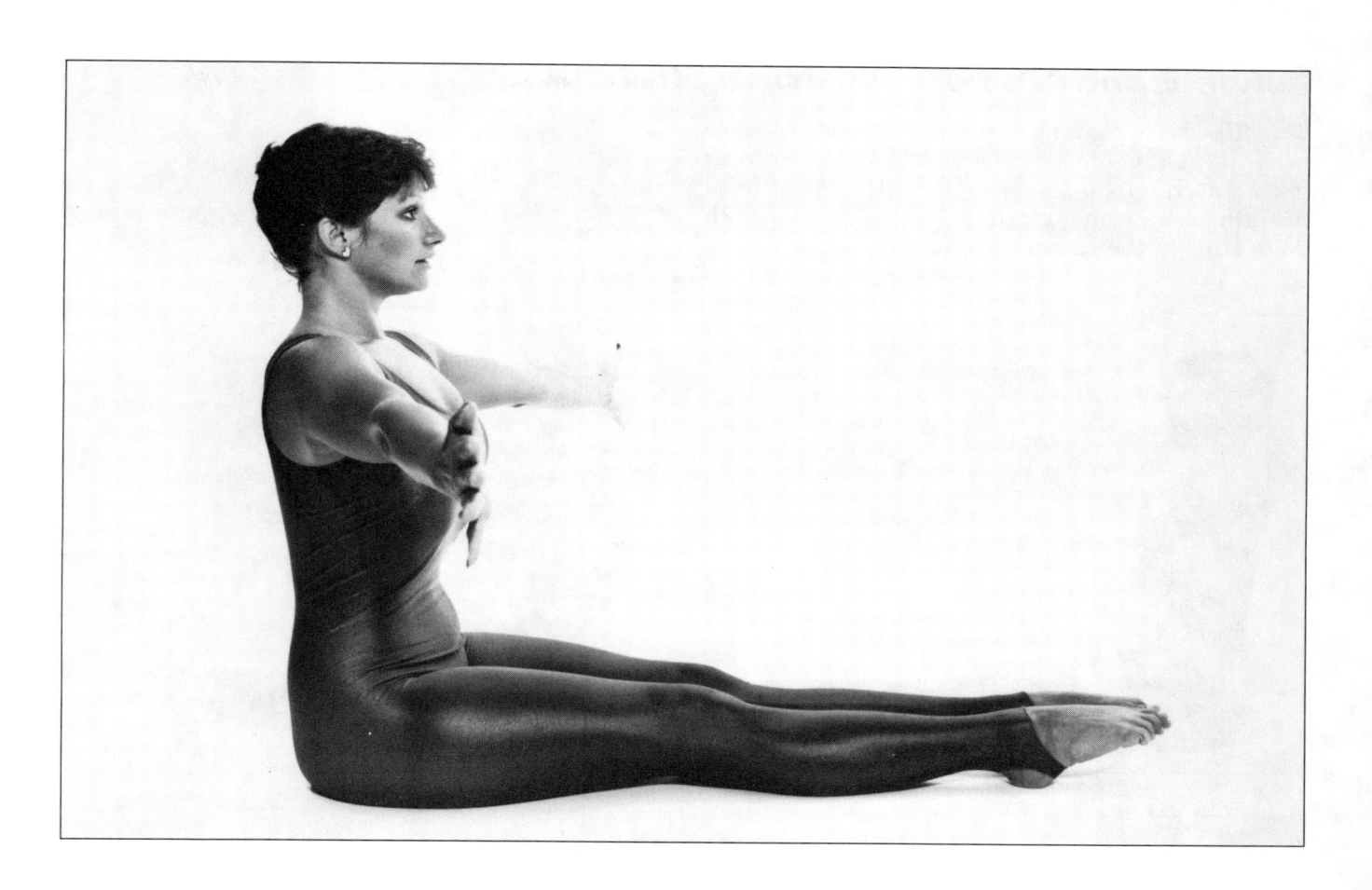

Pelvic Control and Hamstring Stretch

Level III—From a sitting position, perform a forward pelvic tilt. Lift your chest slowly AST straighten your back. Reach forward with a flat back bring arms to the fifth position and return to a sitting position with your arms in the second position.

Pelvic and Abdominal Control

Level I—In a supine position, contract to a sitting position with a flat back bringing knees to your chest. Circle your arms around your legs under hamstrings and extend L leg straight; hold; return leg; repeat R leg.

Level II—Same as above only lift both legs AST into a "V" sit and hold.

Inner Leg and Side Stretch and Strength

Level I—In a supine position, bring your knees to your chest; straddle out; bend your knees and elbows. AST make fist; straighten your legs and point your toes. AST extend your arms to the second position; slowly stretch your torso to the side, leading with your rib cage and return with the same slow stretch; repeat other side. Stretch again, bringing your lead arm in; rotate your trunk to the sky; hold; return; repeat other side.

Note: While in a straddle position, do not roll your knees inward or outward since it puts your body in an improper alignment. Your knees should be facing directly upward.

80 FLOOR EXERCISE TECHNIQUE

Level I—In a straddle position gradually move your trunk forward with the support of your hands; hold; return and repeat.

Level II—In a straddle position, move your trunk forward as far as possible without the support of your hands; then place your hands and stretch with a round back; slowly reach out to a flat back position and return to a sitting position.

Level III—In a straddle position, with your arms overhead and without the support of your hands, move your trunk forward as far as possible; return to an upright position.

Level II—Variation. In a straddle position, lean your trunk forward as far as possible and touch L foot with R hand. Swing to the other side keeping your chest low. Touch R foot with L hand and swing again into a jazz stretch with L hand on the ground and R hand in the air. Repeat other side.

Hip Stretch

Level I—In a swastika position, lean your trunk forward and stretch your hips.

Level II—Same as above, only afterwards stretch your leg by extending your back leg from a swastika position.

Level I—One leg bent over the knee of your other leg. Round your trunk over slowly and hold; roll up and repeat with your other leg.

Level II—Same as before only with both legs bent.

ALL THAT JAZZ AND MORE... 83

Level II—Same as above only after stretching, grab your upper knee with your opposite arm and pull your knee to your chest keeping your hips on the floor; then, pivot your trunk and extend your rib cage up and over three times; come up to a stand; pivot 180° and sit with your other leg to the front; repeat other side.

Hinges for Leg Strength

Level I—In a kneeling position with your knees approximately two feet apart; hinge backwards by lowering as far as possible while maintaining a flat back position; return to an upright position.

Level II—Same as Level I only a hinge position, contract and release pelvic area twice before returning to an upright position.

ALL THAT JAZZ AND MORE... 85

Level III—Hinge back as far as possible; then pelvic tilt backward; arch back and swing arms low. AST execute a body wave to an upright position.

Back Stretch

Level I—In a prone position, place your hands in a push-up position; lift your upper back and release your head back as far as possible; hold and return slowly.

Level II—Same as before only with no hand support.

ALL THAT JAZZ AND MORE... 87

Level III—In a prone position, grasp your ankles and pull up into a swan position; then release your hands and hold.

Level III—In a push up position; grand battement (high kick) back with one leg; bend your knee; twist over backwards and hold; return and repeat.

88 FLOOR EXERCISE TECHNIQUE

Level III—In a jazz split; lift your pelvis from floor and hold; come down into a swastika position; lift into an attitude position on one knee and hold; bring your attitude leg forward into a jazz split on the other side and repeat.

7
Isolation Exercise Technique

The isolation of your hips, torso, head and shoulders, as well as the opposition of these and other body parts, is what makes jazz dance so unique from other forms of dance. Isolation is the separation of a particular part of the body from the whole body for a given movement. The technique used in this exercise section is designed to teach you control of the different anatomical parts used in isolations. For the novice dancer, isolation movement can feel unnatural, but continual use of the isolation technique can result in strong discipline and body control.

The following exercises should begin with eight counts for each movement and diminish to lesser counts of four, two and one, for advanced dancers increase the tempo.

Head

Perform slow head rolls in each direction to warm-up your neck muscles.

Level I—Sharp head turn R; center; L; center. Eliminate center and turn your head alternately R, L, R, L.

ALL THAT JAZZ AND MORE... 91

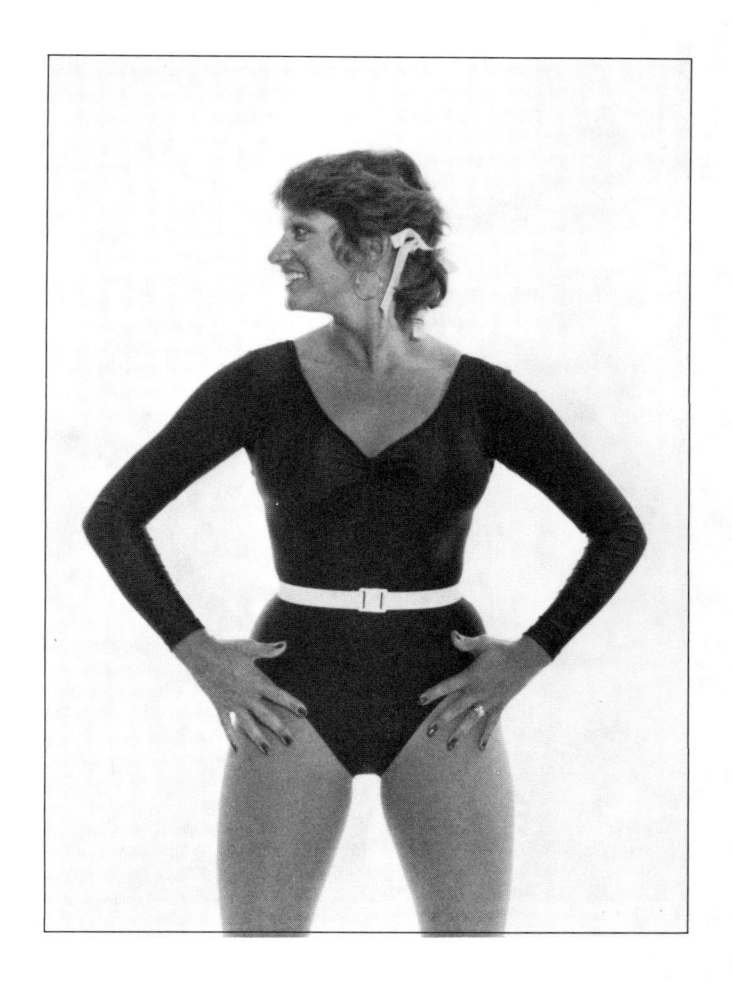

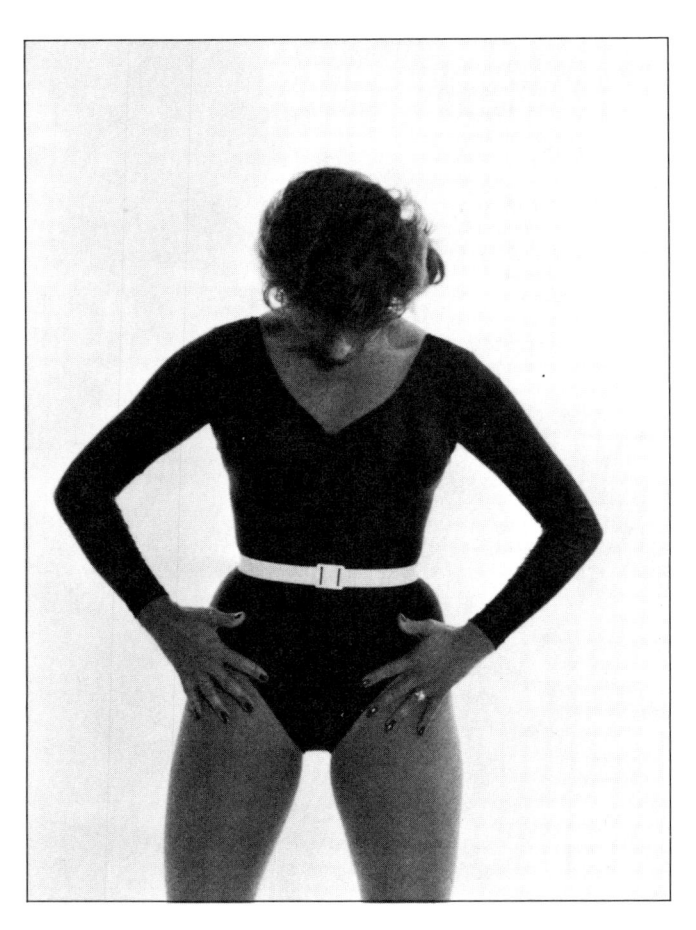

Level I—Sharp head drop forward; center; back; center; then forward, back, forward, back.
Note: Do not extend your head too far backwards; instead maintain control by extending your head only to point of control and comfort.

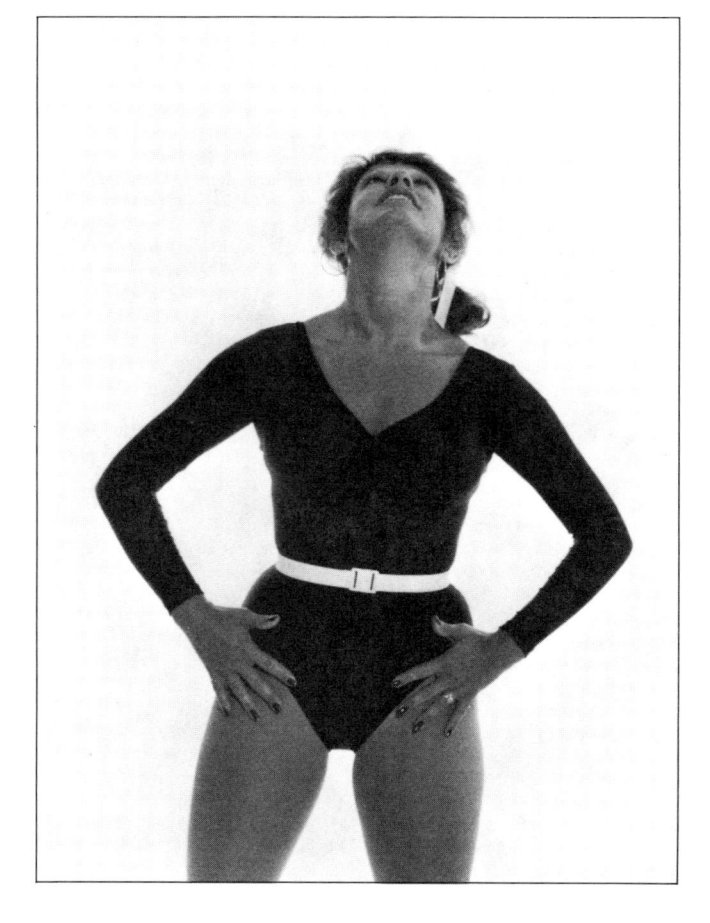

ALL THAT JAZZ AND MORE... 93

Level I—Tilt your head R; center; L; center; then R, L, R, L.
Note: Keep your shoulders pressing down.

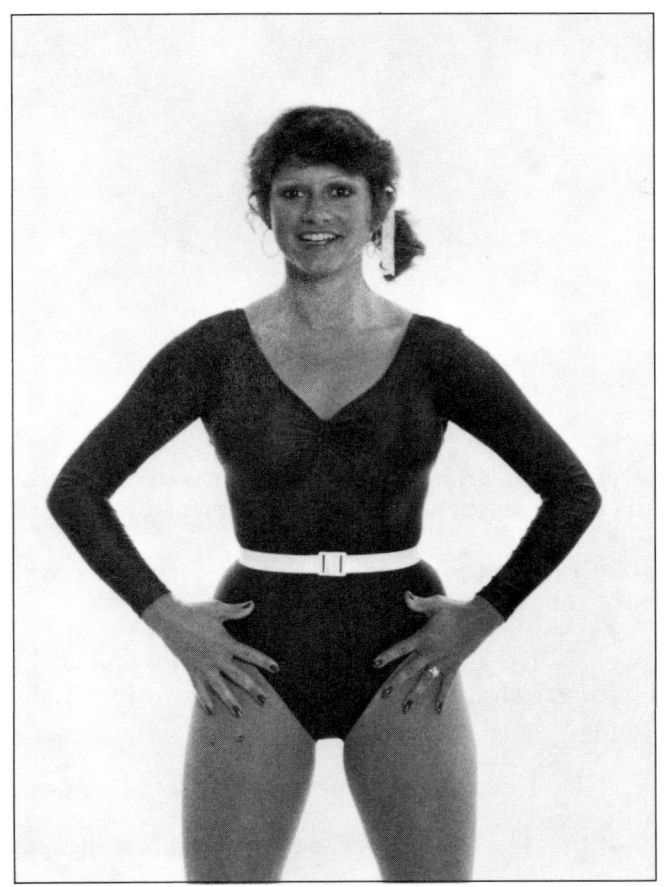

94   ISOLATION EXERCISE TECHNIQUE

Level I—Your head rolls one-half to the R; one-half to the L; then all the way around and reverse.

Level I—Sundari head movements forward and back; side and side; they can also be performed with head rolls.
Note: Pressing your hands against each other will make the movement easier.

Level II—Do all of the aforementioned while walking forward for eight counts and backward for eight counts.

Level III—Head rolls AST perform chassés (see index).

Level III—Head rolls AST perform chaîné turns (see index).

ALL THAT JAZZ AND MORE... 95

Shoulders

Level I—Lift your shoulders up; forward; up; press down into place. Lift your shoulders up; backwards; up and press down again. Repeat while alternating shoulders.

Level I—Shoulder squares; lift your shoulders up, forward, down, and back. Reverse.

Level I—Jazz first position; step R leg to the jazz second position; AST your shoulder comes forward. Return and repeat other side.

Level II—All of the aforementioned; AST walk eight counts forward and eight counts backward.

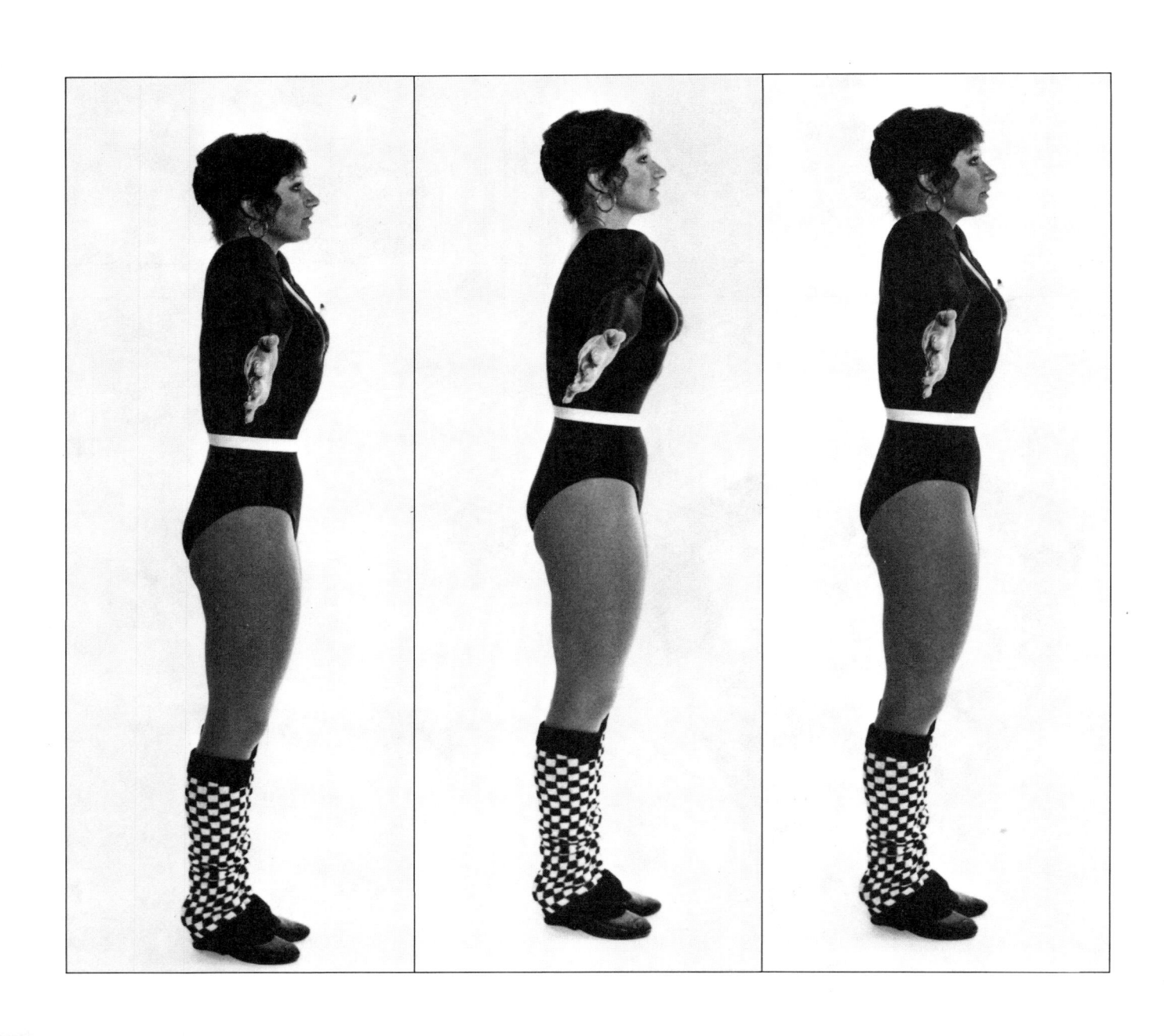

ALL THAT JAZZ AND MORE... 97

ISOLATION EXERCISE TECHNIQUE

Arms

Note: Another term used to describe the carriage of your arms is called "port de bras."

Level I—R arm comes up to a jazz second position; return to a low position first; cross the front of your body; open to the second position; repeat L arm; repeat with both arms simultaneously.

Note: When your arms come down from the second position or a high fifth position, "press" them downwards; your arms should always be firm and under control, yet look relaxed and gentle.

Level II—Alternate your shoulders forward and back while walking with your arms in an upward "V" position.

Level III—Alternate shoulder rolls while walking forward and backward.

Level I—R arm softly comes from a ballet first position to a second position; to a high fifth position, down to your rib cage; "press" out to the second position with a flexed palm; return to a low first position; repeat L arm; repeat both arms.

ALL THAT JAZZ AND MORE... 99

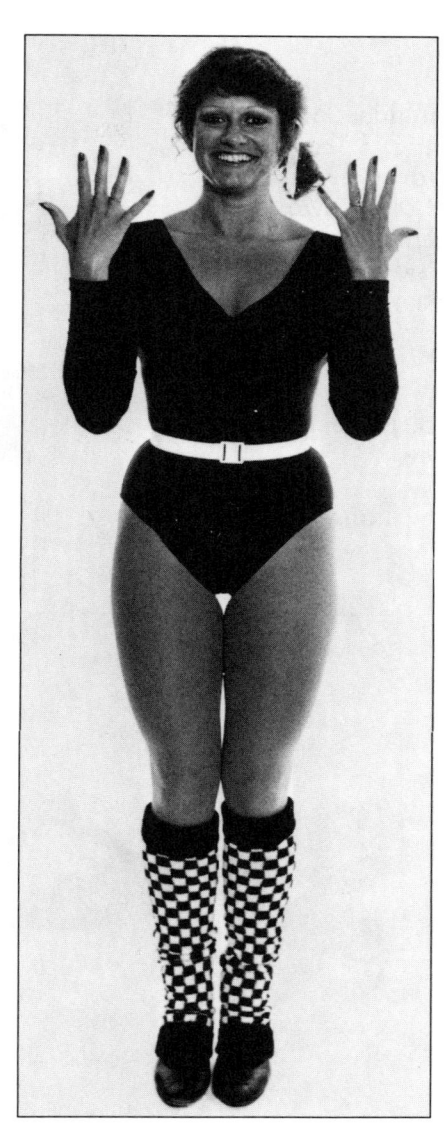

Level I—Bend your arms to your chest with your hands flexed and your elbows sharply in with your palms to back. Straighten sharply to a high fifth position with arms in front; sharply drop your arms to the second position and softly port de bras R arm in an inward circle; return back to the second position and repeat with L arm.
Note: A good idea for individuals who have excess tension in their hands are finger isolations. Try touching each finger with your thumb as you walk, beginning with your little finger and reversing.

Ribs

Level I—Place your hands on your shoulders or on your hips; move your rib cage R, center, L, center taking care not to let your shoulders drop or your hips move. Next move your ribs L, R, L, R. Move your rib cage forward, center, back, center, keeping your stomach lifted and your shoulders down. Then move just forward, back, forward, back. (Imagine your ribs are placed on a table and keep them level as they move from side to side.)

Level II—Move your rib cage forward, R, back, L, then attempt a rib circle motion; reverse.

Level II—Try all of the above while walking.

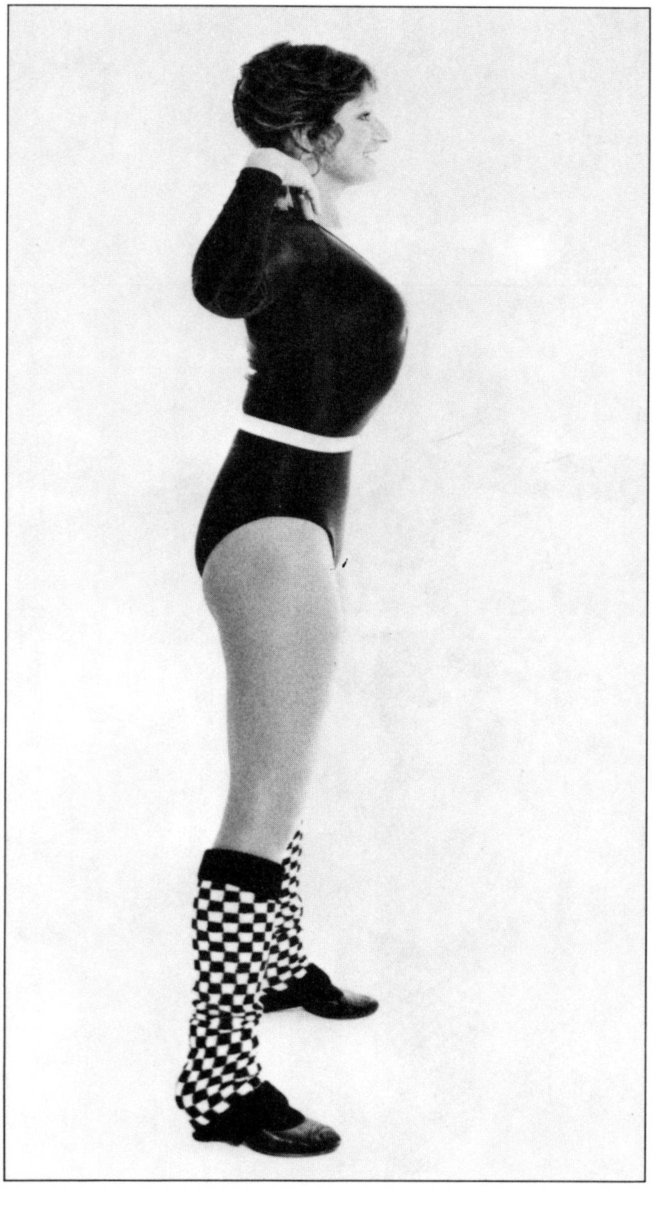

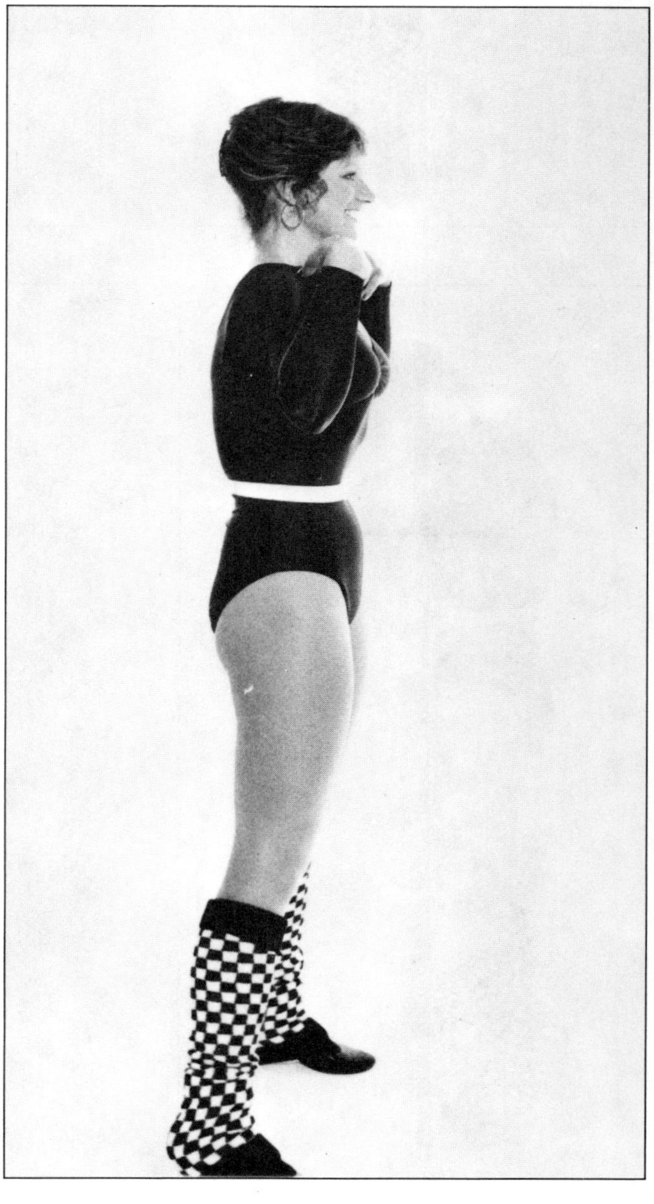

ISOLATION EXERCISE TECHNIQUE

Level II—Jazz second position with your feet and arms; isolate your head, arms and ribs AST; your ribs go R AST your R arm bends in and your head looks R; your ribs go center AST your R hand extends to the second position and your head looks forward; repeat L side; next contract your ribs AST both your arms come in and your head drops forward; release your ribs AST both your arms go out in the second position and your head releases back; reverse the entire combination (L, center, R, center, release and contract).

Level III—Contract-Release Series; step to the jazz second position, AST release your rib cage and head; place your feet together, AST contract your rib cage and lower your head; step one foot behind in a lunge, AST releasing your head and ribs; step feet together in a contracted position again; repeat other side.

Hips

Note: One of the keys to moving your hips freely and easily is to stay in a demi-plié making sure your toes are facing forward. Hip isolations are performed by contracting your inside thigh muscles.

Level I—Jazz feet and hands in the second position demi-plié; move your hips R, center, L, center; then R L R L. Next, move your hips forward, center, back, center; then forward, back, forward, back.

Level II—Try all the aforementioned while walking, AST your arms come from the second position to a high fifth position and back to the second position.

Level I—Move your hips to all four corners; front, R, back, L; then hip roll to the R very slowly and gradually speed up; reverse.

Level II—Hip rolls while performing a chassé (see index) to the side; repeat other side.

106 ISOLATION EXERCISE TECHNIQUE

Level III—Isolate your hips, arms and head AST. Your hip goes R AST your R arm bends in and your head looks R; your hip goes center, AST your arm extends to the second position and your head looks to the center; repeat L side; then your hips go to the front, AST both your arms come in and your head drops; move your hips back, AST your arms go to the second position and your head releases back; reverse entire combination.

Knees

Level I—From the ballet first position, step out to the ballet second position; bend your R knee; rise to your R knee; rise to your toe, keeping the bent knee position then place your heel down; return your feet together and repeat other side.

Level I—From the jazz first position, step out to the jazz second position and simultaneously contract your pelvis and bend your R leg; raise your R foot; your hands are behind your back; return to the first position and repeat other side.

ALL THAT JAZZ AND MORE... 107

Level II—Tendu as before only plantar flex your ankle first, then point the toes of your foot; return to the ball of your foot and return your foot to the first position.

Feet

Level I—From the jazz first position, tendu (point foot forward keeping toe on ground) R forward turned in four times; repeat L side; repeat from the ballet first position forward, side and to the back.

8 KICKS (BATTEMENTS)

Before a good grand battement (big kick) can be attained, you should be flexible in the muscles and joints associated with that particular kick. Therefore, you must focus on the importance of flexibility (see S-T-R-E-T-C-H-ability Chapter). By increasing flexibility in your legs you will enhance your chances for a feeling of accomplishment as well as reduce injuries and strain. Once you have achieved the desired range of motion, you should concentrate both strength and control as demonstrated by the various exercises in this chapter. As a progression to kicks, you should first learn to use your feet correctly. Begin with the "tendu" series as described in the feet section of the Isolation Chapter. After completing that exercise, try this one:

Level I—In the jazz first position; "brush" the floor by pressing against the floor with the ball of your foot until your foot is approximately three inches off the floor. Repeat the brush each time getting higher and higher; repeat opposite foot. Try in the ballet first position; brush forward leading with your heel; brush to the side; brush back. Feel how the brushing effect helps lift your leg off the floor.

When kicking, always keep your legs straight unless otherwise specified. Guard against giving slightly at the small of your back by lifting your rib cage up. Refrain from bending or leaning heavily on your supporting leg. It is very important to establish a center as the source of control and not let your lifted leg pull your hips out of alignment. Watch for tension in your neck and wrists; it is a sign that the center has been lost. Always square your hips and shoulders to the front. Mentally "reach" with your toe if your foot is pointed or with your heel if your foot is flexed. Let your leg do the lifting. Imagine lifting from the muscles underneath. The coming down from a kick should occur because you choose to return to the floor when desired, not because you have to return. To follow these exercise progressions correctly, try getting your leg higher and in more control as the tempo increases.

In summary, the do's and don'ts of a grand battement include:

DO

- Work on flexibility in your legs.
- Use your feet as an aid to lift your leg by "brushing" the floor.
- Square your hips.
- Imagine lifting your leg from underneath.
- Lift your rib cage up while keeping your shoulders down and your body in alignment.
- Keep your legs straight unless otherwise indicated.
- Breathe naturally to avoid tension.
- Point your toes unless otherwise indicated.

DON'T

- Lose control of your arms.
- Bend your supporting leg unless otherwise indicated.

ALL THAT JAZZ AND MORE... 111

- Drop your chest.

- Place unnecessary weight on your supporting hip.

- Look down.

- Get tense.

Développé Stretch

Level II—Passé forward with no turn out; développé leg forward and grasp your ankle or leg with your hand; pull upward; let go and hold that position. Slowly lower your leg. Repeat with your other leg. Repeat développé stretch to the side and back.

Strength Exercise Series

Each movement is performed to two counts.

Level I—In the jazz first position with the second position jazz palms; point your foot AST passé forward and bend your elbows in; développé flexed foot forward as your palms go forward; return to the passé position with your elbows in. Return to the first position and repeat with the other leg.

114 KICKS (BATTEMENTS)

Level I—Same as the aforementioned only développé to the side, AST your arms move to the second position; keep your knees facing upward.

Level I—Same as the aforementioned, only développé backwards, AST your arms go forward; your knee turns toward the floor.

Level II—Passé forward; flex your foot as your leg développés forward; rotate your leg to the side while keeping your hip down; return to passé; return to the first position; repeat bringing your leg from the second développé to the front; repeat bringing your leg from the back to the side; repeat with the other leg.

Level III—All of the aforementioned, on relevé.

Layovers

Level II—In the jazz first position; passé pointed foot forward; then développé with a flexed foot forward; rotate your leg to the side; bend your trunk forward from your waist with a flat back and rotate your knee with the trunk; hold; return to the upright position; return to the passé; then return to the first position; repeat with the other leg.

Level II—In the jazz first position; passé pointed foot forward; then développé with a flexed foot forward; bring your trunk back with a flat back reaching your arms forward; hold; return your trunk, keeping your leg at the same height; passé and return; repeat with the other side.

116 KICKS (BATTEMENTS)

Level II—In the jazz first position; passé your foot forward; développé your flexed foot forward; rotate your leg to the side; reach your trunk and arms to the opposite side; hold; return your trunk; return to passé; return to the first position and repeat with the other side.

Level II—In the jazz first position; passé your pointed foot forward; développé your flexed foot to the side; rotate your leg to the back; bring your trunk forward and stretch into a scale; return your trunk; passé forward; return to the first position; repeat with the other leg.

Level III—All of the aforementioned layovers are done in a relevé position.
Note: All layovers are performed with a stretching effect. As you hold each position, imagine somebody grabbing your heel and another person grabbing your arms, each pulling in opposition. This stretch effect will help you maintain your balance.

Straight Kicks

Level I—From the jazz fourth position, lunge forward with your arms in the jazz second position; kick your back leg forward, AST straightening both legs. Kick four times with your pointed toes; four times with your flexed foot and return to the lunge position after each kick; repeat with the other leg. Variation: Repeat above with a turn-out beginning in the ballet fourth position.

KICKS (BATTEMENTS)

Level I—In the ballet fourth position feet; your arms in the second position; side kick keeping your hips down and your knee to the ceiling; return to the lunge position after each kick; kick four times with your pointed toes and four times with your flexed foot; pivot 360° and repeat with your other leg.

Level I—In the ballet fourth position; your arms in the second position; lunge forward; brush your front foot backward, turning your knee out and making sure your foot is directly behind; return your foot to lunge position after each kick; kick four times with your pointed foot and four times with your flexed foot; repeat with your other leg.

ALL THAT JAZZ AND MORE... 119

Level II—Sideward leg kick; jazz first position; with your trunk bent forward at your hips, your elbows bent, and your wrists crossed; step on your R foot crossing the L foot; kick your L leg to the side; repeat with your other leg.

KICKS (BATTEMENTS)

Plié-Relevé Kicks

Level II—In the jazz first position with the second position jazz palms; kick your R foot front in plié-relevé position; step R foot back in a lunge; step L foot to the second position; step your R foot forward; kick your L foot front in plié-relevé position; step your L foot back; R foot in the second position; L foot forward and repeat. This also can be performed with kicks to the side and back.

Kick Lunges

Level II—In the ballet first position; kick your leg R front with pointed toes returning your leg to a front lunge R turned out; kick R leg front again and return to the ballet first position; repeat kicking side and back while keeping turned out; repeat with your other leg.

122 KICKS (BATTEMENTS)

Attitude Swings

Note: These kicks give freedom of movement of your hips, torso and legs.

Level I—In the ballet first position with the second position jazz arms; tendu (see index) side with R foot; swing your R leg across your body into an attitude front; return swing across your body to an attitude side; swing your R leg again across your body and continue a complete inward rotation; reverse by swinging your leg outward; inward; rotate your leg outward ending in an attitude side; place your foot in the ballet first position; repeat other side.

ALL THAT JAZZ AND MORE... 123

Level III—Same as above; only everytime your leg swings across your body relevé on the supporting leg.

Level II—Same as above, only every time your leg swings across your body, demi-plié to create an up and down rhythm.

Fan Kicks

Level II—In the ballet second position with the second position jazz arms; brush your leg in an outward circle from your hip with a straight leg and end by lunging in back. Perform an inward fan kick rotation by rotating your straight leg inward and ending in a side lunge. Make sure your knee is in a turned out position in all rotations. The rotation is done in front of your body and your supporting leg is either straight or in a plié-relevé position; repeat with your other leg. Variation: Turn 180° in middle of a fan kick.

Arched Kick Out

Level III—In the ballet first position with long, low jazz arms; kick with toe pointed to the second position extending your leg outward as you kick and arch your back. Place your foot down; and wrap your arms around body.

Hitchkick

Level II—Small lunge forward with your L foot forward and turned out; kick your R leg up and switch your L leg forward in flight, land on your R leg first; repeat other with your leg. This can be done to the front, side or back.

9 Locomotive Movements

Locomotor movements, or total body motion, require quick weight shifting and concentrated centering. I recommend that you initially concentrate on obtaining an overview of the total locomotive section.

Then as you learn these steps and movements, learn them in this order; 1) Concentrate on successfully completing your foot movements. 2) Concentrate on learning the arm motions along with the foot movements. 3) Work on your hips. 4) Work on your head and any other body part. Don't try to learn everything at once. Always maintain good posture and eye contact. Never look down; instead, look directly where you are going.

Make sure you have the proper techniques before progressing. Not only will these techniques give you the strength and consistency you'll need for dancing, but they will enable you to dance longer by reducing your chance of being injured.

To perform, have enough space to cover at least twenty-four counts of walks. And remember, technique becomes exciting when you give it meaning and expression.

Jazz Walks

The first most important step is to be able to walk to the count of the music beat. Begin by just walking across the floor stepping with the beat of the music. Count by counts of eight (1,2,3,4,5,6,7,8,1,2...). Now try half counting to the music. Step on every two counts (1,3,5...). Let's go a little faster and step twice to every beat while you count out loud (1&2&3&4&5...). As you advance, you will be able to go from one rhythm to another without stopping.

Notice as you walk naturally that your arms swing in opposition. You will notice that most walks and jazz movements are done in opposition unless otherwise specified by the choreographer. Begin on the first count of eight and if you are in a class situation, the next person should wait eight counts before walking.

All walks are Level I; you can speed up the tempo for Levels II and III. All walks have optional arms; however, for a beginner, it is best to keep your arms low and slightly back. Remember to keep your chest and stomach lifted and, of course, your eye contact forward.

Walks with Isolations

BASIC WALK—Walk forward four counts; stop and move your hips R, L, R, L on every count; repeat double time.

Variation—Move your hips while walking at the same time; step R and move your hip to R; step L and move your hip to L; do the same with your shoulders, head and ribs as described in the Isolation Chapter.

Variation—Port de bras (see index) your arms while walking as described in Isolaton Chapter.

128 LOCOMOTIVE MOVEMENTS

HIP WALK—Leading with your knee and hip, walk forward with slightly bent knees, keeping toes forward (your knees should almost touch when passing each other).

ALL THAT JAZZ AND MORE... 129

BACK HIP WALK—Your hips push to the back as you step forward in a demi-plié; keep your toes forward and your trunk slightly forward; optional arms—wiggle your fingers in jazz hands.

INWARD HIP WALK—In demi-plié leading with your hip, walk forward turning your front foot inward as you step; your body turns slightly to the side in the direction of the leading foot.

LOW JAZZ WALK—Demi-plié your toes forward; roll from your heel to the ball of your foot as you step forward; keep your palms open, your arms in opposition, and your trunk upright; be sure to keep low and level.

AFRO JAZZ WALK—Same as low jazz walk only with your trunk forward.

ALL THAT JAZZ AND MORE... 131

TOE DRAG WALK—Step forward in a demi-plié, drag your back foot keeping your leg straight and sliding on side of your big toe; your shoulders alternate slightly; repeat with your other leg.

BACK HIP ROLL WALK—While walking backwards, contract, lift and release your hips in a roll between each step. Demi-plié with your toes forward.

CHARACTER WALK—Facing to the side, your elbows in and jazz hands out; look over your slightly lifted shoulder; leading with your rib cage, lean back and walk to the side crossing one foot over the other every other step.

BOUNCE WALK—Relevé your foot as you step forward; your other foot steps flat forward in a demi-plié; repeat.

134 *LOCOMOTIVE MOVEMENTS*

TAP WALK—Tap your R foot next to your L foot by hitting the floor with the ball of your foot; step forward on your R foot in a demi-plié; bring your L foot to the R and tap as your R knee straightens; step with your L foot forward in a demi-plié; repeat.

ALL THAT JAZZ AND MORE... 135

TAP LUNGES—Same as the tap walk, only instead of stepping forward, lunge forward while turning your foot inward and leading with your shoulders.

STEP TOUCHES—The opposite of tap walks. Step forward on your R foot, bringing L foot to the R and touching your foot beside it; repeat with your other leg.

CROSS TOUCH WALK—Demi-plié with your feet parallel; crossing your R foot over your L foot, touch your L foot to the side with a fully extended leg and a pointed leg and a pointed toe; repeat to other side.

ALL THAT JAZZ AND MORE... 137

CROSSOVER WALKS—Cross one foot over the other while in a turned-out demi-plié; your opposite shoulder comes with one hand on your hip and your other hand in the second position with a jazz palm.

PASSÉ WALK BACK—Walk backwards lifting your leg in the passé position turned in before stepping. After eight counts, repeat with your knee in passé turned out.

138 LOCOMOTIVE MOVEMENTS

FRENCH TWIST WALK—Lift your knee to the passé inward position crossing your other foot on relevé while keeping your legs straight; step on the lifted foot and repeat with your other side.

ATTITUDE TWIST WALK—Step R in a demi-plié; AST lifting your L leg in a back attitude and twisting to the R as far as possible; step L leg forward in a demi-plié and an attitude R; repeat.

SIDE WALK—Begin facing to the side; step with your R foot to the R side; lean your hip to the L; stepping L to R with your hip leaning to the R; repeat.

SIDE WALK WITH PARTNER—Repeat as before only with two people facing each other and performing in opposition AST as if mirroring each other.

MIRROR WALK—Facing partner; mirror each other's arms as they come from the first position to the second position to high fifth then back to first while walking side the entire time.

140 LOCOMOTIVE MOVEMENTS

HIP LIFT WALK—Walk four steps forward; lift your R hip for two counts with your arms in the third position; extend your hip for two counts, AST arch your back; your arms drop to the second position; place your hip down for two counts and repeat.

CAMEL WALK—Step forward on your R heel; roll to the ball of your foot, AST you roll your hips forward; finish with your L foot coming to the R; repeat.

AFRO-JAZZ VARIATION—Same as before only your trunk is in a forward position.

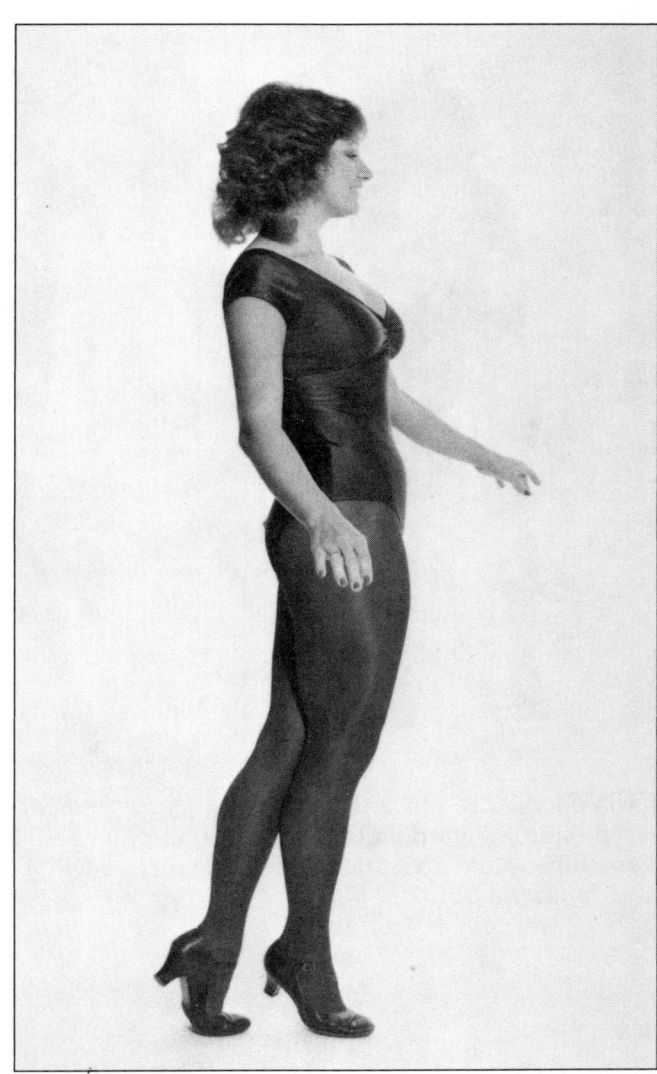

142 LOCOMOTIVE MOVEMENTS

CUBAN WALK—In a demi-plié with your feet forward; step forward to the R; then L in place, AST your hips make a figure eight; walk forward R, L, and repeat.

SPANISH WALK—Four hip walks forward; step R foot forward in small lunge as your body pivots to the L and your L arm comes up. Place your R hand on your hip with your R shoulder slightly raised; pivot 180° and walk again.

ALL THAT JAZZ AND MORE... 143

FOUR CORNERS WALK—Walk four steps forward; make a one-half circle with your R hip and knee beginning from the bottom of the circle to the top, then back down from the top to the bottom. AST your R heel comes off the floor and returns back. Reverse with your other hip and walk four steps again; repeat.

144 LOCOMOTIVE MOVEMENTS

TWIST KICK WALK—Step R, L, R, then L together; twist your hips in place R, L, R and on the last L twist perform a small kick with your L foot. Walk three steps and repeat with your other side.

JAZZ RUN—Staying low to the ground, perform large lunges while running and sliding your back leg on the side of your large toe. Turn your feet out; place your arms in opposition. When the run is perfected, try alternating your shoulders.

TRAVELING KICKS—Any type kicks can be done traveling. (See Kick Chapter for more details.) Try alternating kicks one after the other and if the music is too fast, walk three counts between kicks.

TRAVELING TURNS—See next chapter for turns and their progressions.

Basic Jazz Steps

The following are for any level unless otherwise specified. Add arm variations and speed for more advanced levels.

BALL CHANGE—Transfer your weight from one foot to another with the ball of your foot, then the entire foot. This can be done in any direction.

STEP BALL CHANGE—Step R forward; switch from the ball of one foot to the ball of your other foot—L, R in place. This should be done in the following manner: full foot, ball of foot, and full foot; then repeat using your other side.

146 LOCOMOTIVE MOVEMENTS

KICK BALL CHANGE—Small kick with R foot; place your R foot behind your L foot and change from the ball of one foot to the ball of your other foot—R, L in place; repeat with your other side.

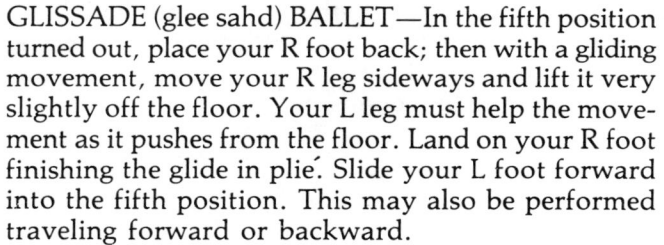

GLISSADE (glee sahd) BALLET—In the fifth position turned out, place your R foot back; then with a gliding movement, move your R leg sideways and lift it very slightly off the floor. Your L leg must help the movement as it pushes from the floor. Land on your R foot finishing the glide in plie´. Slide your L foot forward into the fifth position. This may also be performed traveling forward or backward.

GLISSADE JAZZ—Same as before only starting from the jazz first position and end by crossing your R leg over your L leg.

148 LOCOMOTIVE MOVEMENTS

CHASSÉ (shah-say) JAZZ—Step, together, step (example: step R to R; step L next to R; step R to R again); done in a 1 & 2 rhythm; either done ball, ball, flat or flat, ball, flat. This is performed in plié-relevé position leading with your hips; it may however be done in various directions.

CHASSÉ BALLET—From the fifth position, place your foot forward and slide your R leg forward in demi-plié. From this position, push both your legs up from the floor to meet in the air in a tightly pressed fifth position. To finish, your back leg should land in a plié while your R leg immediately slides forward in a demi-plié ready to spring up again.

ALL THAT JAZZ AND MORE... 149

CHUGS—Traveling in the air while hopping on one foot.

SISSONNE (see sohn)—Leave the floor with both feet, but land on one foot.

GRAPEVINE—Facing to the side; step your R foot to the side; your L foot crosses behind your R foot; step your R foot to the side; your L foot crosses in front of your R foot; keep repeating.

PAS DE BOURRÉE (pah deh boo-ray)—These three steps can be performed in many directions. In the plié-relevé position; cross your L foot behind your R; step with your R foot to the R side; step with your L foot to the front; flat, ball, flat; always staying low making sure not to come up in the middle of the step. This can be done to a single or a half-count but should not be confused with a step ball change as the rhythm is different (Level II).

TURNING PAS DE BOURRÉE—Either turn one-quarter, one-half, or full while doing a back, side, front foot movement as explained before. Begin turning on the second step and "spot" before you finish your third step. (Level II.)

JUMPING PAS DE BOURRÉE—Take off on the first step with a jump, then complete the pas de bourrée as described before. (Level II).

JAZZ SQUARE—Steps are taken in a square floor pattern. On your R foot step across in front of your L foot; step back on your L foot; step to the R side on your R foot; step forward on your L foot. This can be done with either foot leading. Variation: Replace the third step with a chassé followed by a step forward on the L, cross step on your R foot and a chassé to the L.

JAZZ SHOOT—The footwork is almost the same as the Jazz Square, but there is an additional chug. On your R foot step across in front of your L foot; chug back on your R foot; step back on your L foot; step to the R on your R foot and step forward on your L foot.

LINDY—Really a chassé ball change. Step together, step (R, L, R) to the R, step back on the ball of your L foot; step forward on your R foot, repeat other side.

152 LOCOMOTIVE MOVEMENTS

SUGAR FOOT—Step on the ball of your R foot with your knee turned out, then pivot on your R foot so that your R knee turns in. Step forward to the L, your knee turned out; pivot with your knee rotating inward. The pivot and the next step may be done simultaneously. (Switch hips as you travel and shake hands.)

SUZY Q—Standing in the first position parallel, turn your toes to the R. Still moving to the R, turn both heels to the R, then your toes again, heels etc. This step is done as a Charleston variation.

154 LOCOMOTIVE MOVEMENTS

UNCLE WIGGILY—Begin standing with your weight on both feet, your legs rotated inward. Pivot on the ball of your L foot, and the heel of your R foot, so that your toes end rotated outward. Then pivot on the ball of your R foot, and the heel of your L foot AST and end with your toes turned inward. These series of movements travel in the same direction.

VARSITY DRAG—Lift your R knee, AST touch your R knee with the palms of your hands; step back to the R; step L to the side; step to the R across in front of your L. Repeat on your opposite side.

SKATE—Pivot your body to the R for two counts as your shoulder leads and your hip goes in opposition like a skating effect; repeat on your other side for two counts, then single count in each direction.

SHUFFLE—In the jazz first position; on each count your feet alternately go forward as far as possible keeping one foot on the ground and accenting each time your foot comes in. Your knees should bend slightly everytime your leg comes in; "a shuffling of the feet."

156 LOCOMOTIVE MOVEMENTS

NEW YORKER—Step forward with your R foot AST lift your foot off the floor; step L in place picking up your R foot; step on R behind your L foot AST lift your L foot off the ground; step L in place again; lead with your shoulders.

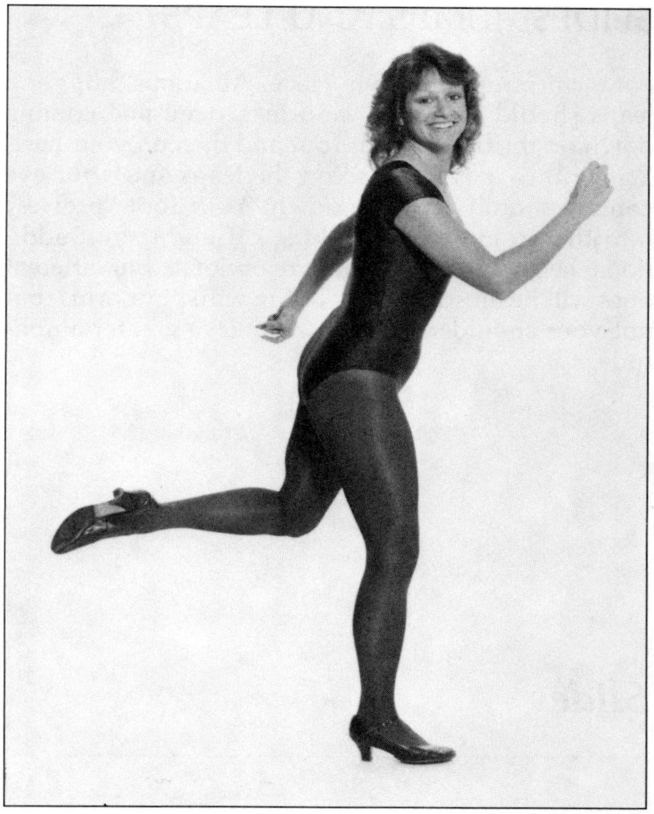

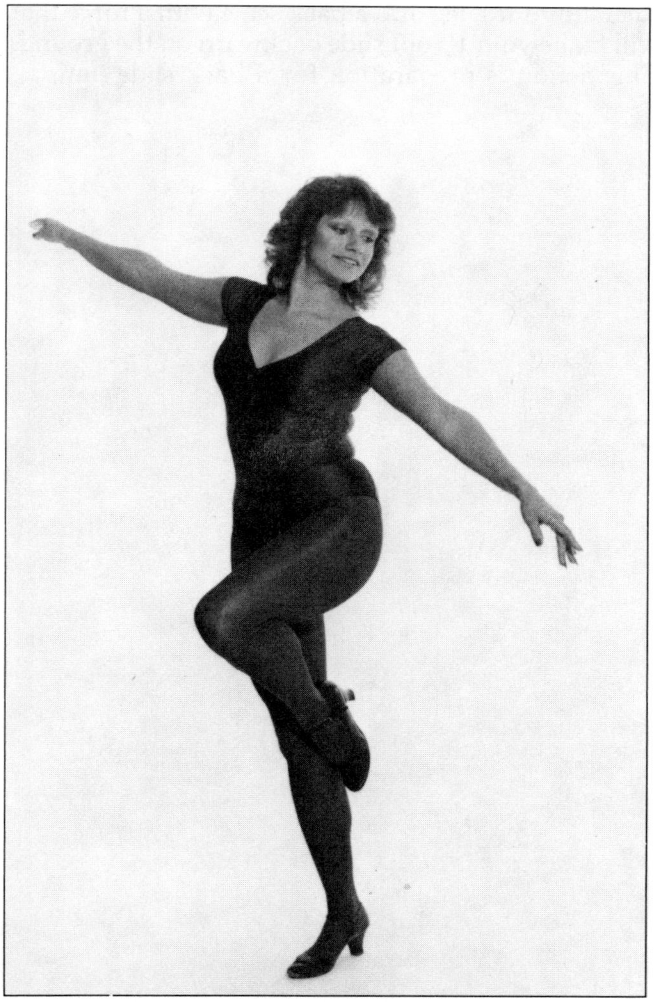

SLIDES, JUMPS AND LEAPS

For a warm-up, prance in place. All jumps, hops and leaps should start and land in a demi-plié coming down on the ball of your foot and then on your heel. Your rib cage is forward on the leaps and your eye contact should never be down. Your foot "presses" into the ground before taking off giving you additional height. Arm positions are optional, but different ones will be illustrated. By lifting with your arms (but not your shoulders), you can achieve greater amplitude.

Slides

Level II—BACK SLIDE—In a jazz first position, step your R foot back as your arms cross at your wrists; then lift your L leg into a back scale with a force that will make your R foot slide backward on the ground. This action is preparation for a back slide jump.

Level I—SIDE SLIDE—Cross your L leg over your R leg in a demi-plié; large lunge to the R by pushing hard with your L foot; AST slide your L foot towards your R foot until it crosses over your R foot again; this slide can be done in any direction with different hip positions (always slide on the outside of your big toe).

Jumps

Level I—JAZZ JUMP—Run forward R, L and hop on your R foot bringing your L foot to a forward passé position. Land on your R foot and repeat with your other side.
Note: The hop should take two counts while in the air. This action is preparation for a jazz jump turn.

Level II—JAZZ JUMP TURN—Repeat as before only rotate 180° while in the air and continue running backwards.

160 LOCOMOTIVE MOVEMENTS

Level I—ARABESQUE JUMP—Run toward R, L and jump up onto your R foot bringing your L foot back to an arabesque position while in the air.

Level I—ATTITUDE JUMP—Same as before only bring your L foot backward in an attitude position while in the air.
Variation—Put your leg in a *forward* attitude.

ALL THAT JAZZ AND MORE... 161

Level II—ARCHED JUMP—Run forward R, L; step with your feet together, and jump up to a back arched position with your head leaning back; spot to the front. Come down with your feet together; repeat with your other side with your L leg leading; this action is preparation for double stag jump.

Level I—STRAIGHT JUMP—Run forward R, L, step with your feet together and jump straight into the air; stay in the air for two counts and come down with both of your feet together; repeat with your L leg leading; this action is preparation for the arched jump.

162 LOCOMOTIVE MOVEMENTS

Level III—DOUBLE STAG JUMP—Run R, L, step with your feet together and jump up into the air splitting your legs and touching the toes on your right foot to your L knee and the toes of your left foot to your head; land on your R foot.

Level II—JACKKNIFE (CABRIOLE)—Cross your R foot over your L leg in demi-plié; push off your R foot while you lift your L leg to the side; tap your R foot to your L foot while in the air; come down on your R foot. This can also be done forward in a turned-out position.
Variation: STAG JACKKNIFE—Tap your foot to your L knee while in the air.

Level II—RIGHT ANGLE JUMP WITH A SLIDE—Cross your R leg over your L leg in a demi-plié; your arms are crossed at your wrists. Lift your L leg to a 90° angle, AST you push off to the R into a hop with your arms going out to the second position.
Note: Your arm swing will give you an extra "lift."

Level II—BACK SLIDE JUMP—This is the same as the back slide, only instead of sliding your R foot on the ground, push off your R foot into the air.

Variation: BACK SLIDE STAG JUMP—Your R foot touches your L knee while in the air.

164 LOCOMOTIVE MOVEMENTS

Level II—BARREL TURN JUMP—Step to the side with a R lead as a preparation; push off to the R and turn 360° outside (to the L); make a barrel type turn; your legs can be either straight or bent in an attitude position; face forward as long as possible during the turn.

Level II—FOUETTÉ (fwer rā) BATTEMENT—Stand in the fifth position with your foot forward; kick your R foot forward in a grand battement, AST push with your L foot so that your body is off the ground. Turn your body 180° to the L, ending in an arabesque with your R leg to the rear. This is usually preceded by a chassé or glissade (see index) in order to get the necessary momentum.

Level II—TOURJETE (tōre shet tā)—This is a jumping turn. Stand in the fifth position, with your R foot forward; kick your R leg, AST push off the ground with your L leg; quickly change legs AST your body turns 180°. Land on your R leg in a scale with your L leg extended to the back in an arabesque.

ALL THAT JAZZ AND MORE... 165

Leaps

Level I—STRAIGHT LEAP—Run forward R, L, take off on your R foot into the air in a split position; land on your R foot. Begin with a low split and try to go higher and higher on each leap. Beginners should attempt this with their hands on their shoulders; their arms can be in the second, fourth or high fifth positions. This action is preparation for a stag leap.

Level III-BACK STAG LEAP—Bend your back leg instead of your front leg, while keeping your front leg straight with your back foot reaching for your head as your head is dropped backwards; land on your front leg.

Level II—STAG LEAP—Same as before only while in the air extend your back leg, AST bend your forward knee so that your foot touches the knee of your extended leg. Land on your front leg.
Variation: While in a split leap, open your legs to a straight leg split leap before landing.

Level III—ONE-HALF TURNING STAG LEAP—While performing a stag leap, turn your body 180° in the air, drop your front leg to land and continue running backwards.

Level II—SECOND POSITION LEAP—Leap to the side with your body facing forward and both your legs in the second position while in flight. Variation: Stag one leg during leap.

Level III—CHAINÉ LEAPS—(See Turn Chapter on Chainé Turns.) Chainé two steps and instead of stepping on the third step as described in the Turn Chapter, leap forward. Chainé turns are done in a demi-plié position so as to give more lift on the leap. Your working leg extends straight to the side, not around in a fan kick. Try combining the two or three jumps you have just learned.

10 FLOORWORK

You need to increase the area of impact or the time of impact to absorb the force of impact gradually. On falls, try to carry them out smoothly and quietly. Avoid landing on your knees, elbows, the coccyx or the tip of your shoulders. Control your weight so that mass of your body is as close to the floor as possible and attempt to slide to the floor instead of landing hard in one spot. You can lessen the impact by bending your elbows and cushioning the force with your hands.
Note: Use falls with caution if you have any special problem areas that might be susceptible to injury.

Level I—PROGRESSION FOR FRONT FALL—Begin in a kneeling position with your arms extended forward and your palms flexed; fall forward with a straight back, giving at your elbows to cushion the fall.

Level II—FRONT FALL—From a jazz second position, bend slightly forward from the trunk with your arms extended forward and your palms flexed. Fall forward with a straight back and land in a push-up type position bending at your elbows. Make sure that you control your chest when lowering yourself to the floor.

Level II—SWEDISH FALL—Same as before only with one leg extended back into an arabesque as you are falling. This is also done with a slight body arch to ease the fall. Your chest touches the floor first.

ALL THAT JAZZ AND MORE... 171

Level II—SLIDE FALL—Cross your L foot over your R leg bringing your arms up overhead and leaning towards the direction of the fall (to the R). Keeping your arms reaching above your head to lessen the impact of your fall; continue bending your R knee until on the R side of your thigh; then straighten body out on floor.

Level II—BACK FALL—Contract forward and drop your chin as you bring one foot back; lower your trunk until hands touch the floor; then sit back on your posterior and straighten your body out to a supine position on the floor.

Level III—SHOULDER ROLL—Deep lunge to the R. With your arms in the second position, curl your R shoulder forward and lean on the R side of your body. Roll over to a second position split and continue rolling over while bending your L knee. Come up to a knee lunge with your arms in the second position. This is usually preceded by a chassé or cross slide to give momentum.

Level III—PARTNER SHOULDER ROLL—Lunge R as before, but next to a partner who is in a bent trunk stance position. Instead of rolling over the floor, roll over your partner's back.

Level II—JAZZ SPLIT SLIDE—Run forward R, L, R; slide onto the ground with your L leg forward and straight balancing the weight on the L side of your foot; lift your hips up and travel on your slide as much as possible; your R leg is bent in the jazz split position. Your body leans slightly onto your L side. During the slide, your L hand reaches for the ground and "pushes" away when it touches the ground giving you more momentum. This action is preparation for the split side series.

ALL THAT JAZZ AND MORE... 175

Level III—SPLIT SLIDE SERIES—Same as before only keep your back leg straight so you are in a split leg position. After sliding, roll onto your stomach, then return to a supine position with your knees bent and your feet slightly apart. Perform a body roll up to a standing position.

Level II—KNEE ROLLS—Begin on your knees, with your R leg; turn to the L 360°, bringing your knees together and lift your L knee up at the end of the turn. The position of your arms is optional but your arms can help the rotation when they begin in the second position, then close to the fifth position during the turn, and finally return to a second position to help stop the turn.

ALL THAT JAZZ AND MORE... 177

Level III—SPLIT SERIES—Begin in a R split position with your arms in the second position; squeeze your legs together and bring your arms up to a high fifth position lifting your body up and around 180° to a L split position.
Note: Do not attempt unless you have a good second position split.

GYMNASTICS

Because of a lack of space, gymnastics cannot be adequately treated in this book. There are many good books on the market today on gymnastics—so I'll leave gymnastics to the specialists in the field. Sometimes gymnastics is referred to as acrobatics in the dance world. Tumbling or floor exercise would be a better term as the skills used in dance do not require the gymnastics events that include equipment.

A list of gymnastics skills prominent in jazz dance today includes the following:

Forward Roll and Variations
Backward Roll and Variations

Cartwheel
One Handed Cartwheel

Handstand
Aerial Cartwheel

Front Walkover and Variations
Back Walkover and Variations
Round-off
Barani
Back Handspring or Flip Flop
Front and Back Flips and Variations

COMBINATIONS

Try to put the skills listed in this chapter and the Locomotive Chapter together to form a dance combination concentrating on fluidity. As in gymnastics, a round-off is incomplete without a back handspring. Accordingly, dance moves intertwine and give energy to each other. Remember, don't sacrifice technique to make it through a combination. Beginning jazz combinations should be kept simple with the emphasis on clean technique and repetition. Start slowly and progress to a faster tempo.

11 TURNS

A well admired teacher of mine once gave me some good advice. "If you are ever going to learn how to turn, you have to imagine yourself having one leg, one leg only, and as you attempt the turn be assertive on that one leg. If you should fall, fall big!"

Now that doesn't mean for you to crash and break your neck. However, do not just fumble through a turn by occasionally tapping the other foot for support. On a one-footed turn, keep your other leg lifted as long as possible. And if you are trying to turn around twice on one leg, think six! Chances are you will do more than you had expected.

There are two important "secrets" to performing a successful turn. These two secrets are the key to turning, whether you are attempting a beginning double leg turn or an advanced one legged turn six times. The first key is what dancers call "spotting." Spotting is a method of being able to execute a number of turns without getting dizzy. It also helps you find your balance and "center" and can assist you in starting and stopping the rotation. A good way to learn spotting is to focus your eyes forward (without lifting or dropping the chin) at a natural level and at a specific object—real or imagined—on a wall or in space. Begin rotating your body in a circle, keeping your eyes focused on the object until you cannot hold it anymore. When you have reached the point where you body is turned as far as it can with your head still unmoved, snap your head around, in a complete rotation as quickly as possible letting your body follow. In other words, in a turn, your head is the last part of your body to leave and the first to return. Gradually increase the speed of turning and continue doing as many times as you can. Now try the opposite direction.

The second secret to turning is arm control. Arms vary in jazz dancing, depending on the type of turn, but there is a standard arm position used if you are just learning how to turn. It is called an "open-close-open" position. "Open" refers to the second position jazz or ballet arms and "close" refers to the ballet fifth en avant position arms. By closing to the fifth position in the middle of a turn, you are shortening your radius, thus gaining more momentum and speed. Try closing your eyes and *feeling* the "open-close-open" position as you go through the motions. By controlling your arms, they can assist you in a turn. But flyaway arms can throw you from your center, thus causing you to fall forward, backwards or even to the side.

ALL THAT JAZZ AND MORE... 181

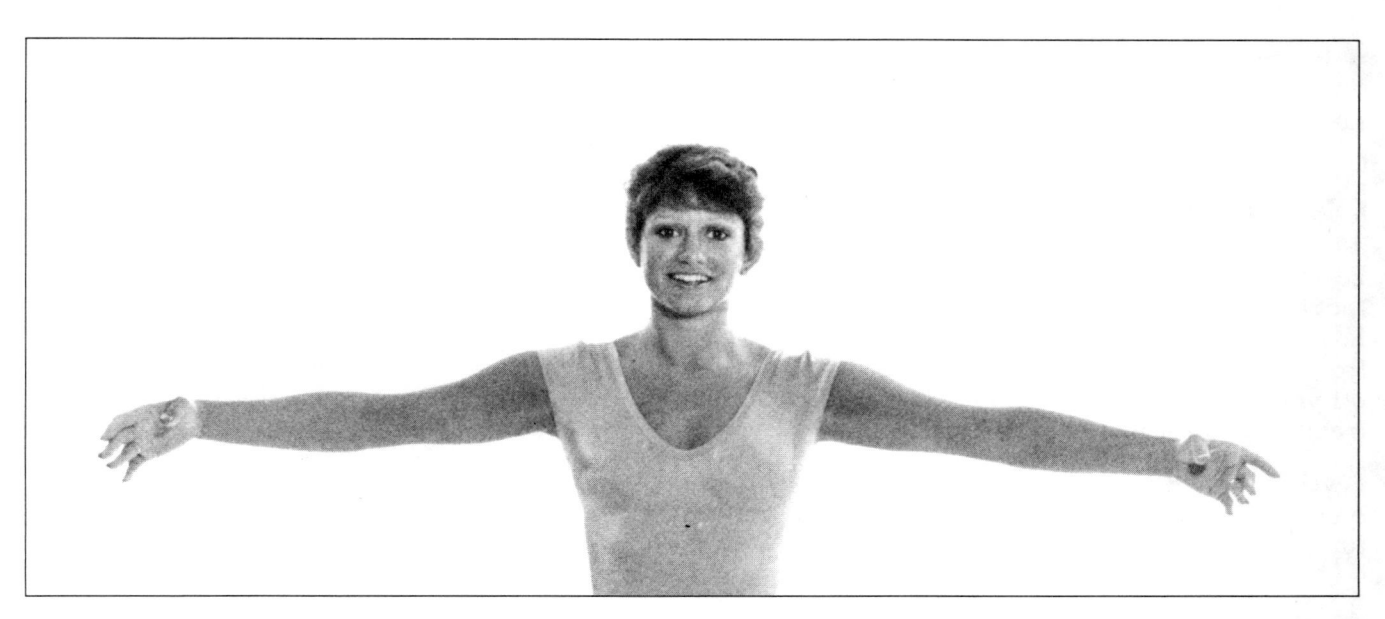

Two-Footed Turns

Let's begin with the easiest turn—the one-half turn:

ONE-HALF TURN

Level I—In the jazz first position; step with your R foot front and lift your L foot. AST pivot 180° to the L; step on the L foot and bring your R foot to the front again and repeat. Lead with your hip and roll off your back foot when stepping to the front; spot front and repeat with your other side.

Level I—VARIATION—Walk R, L, R, L, step R and one-half turn as before; step R again and one-half turn; repeat across the floor.

THREE STEP TURN

Level I—PROGRESSION—In the jazz first position with the second position jazz arms; step R to R on count one; cross L over R on count two; step R to R on count three; touch L next to R on count four, AST clap your hands together. Repeat with your other side. Practice spotting by moving your head sharply on the first count to the R if going R and to the L if going L.

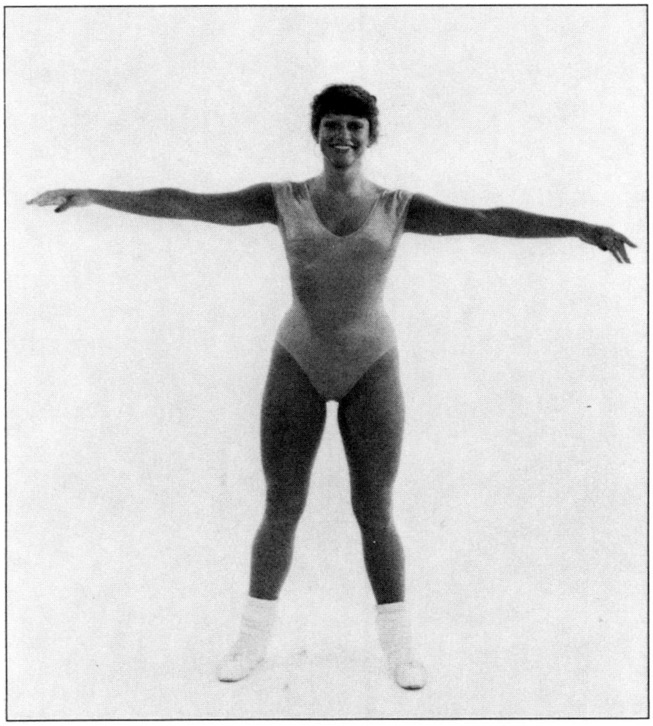

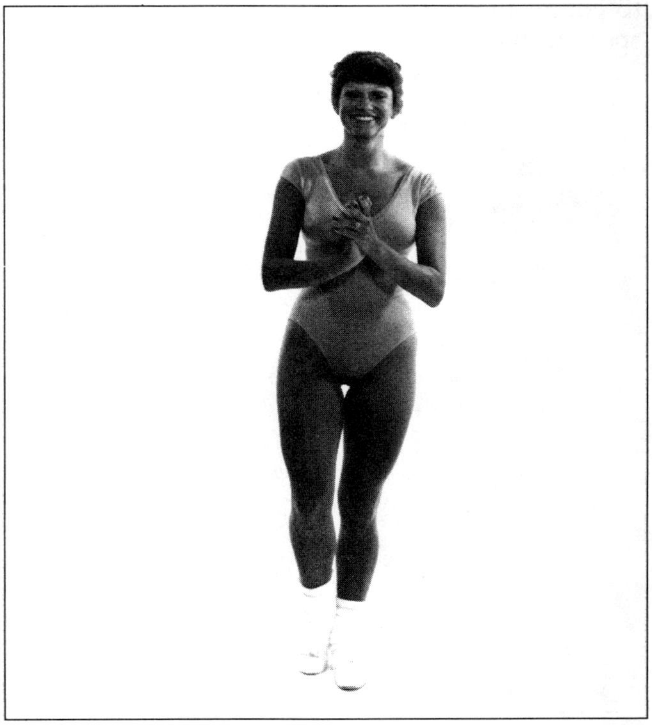

184 TURNS

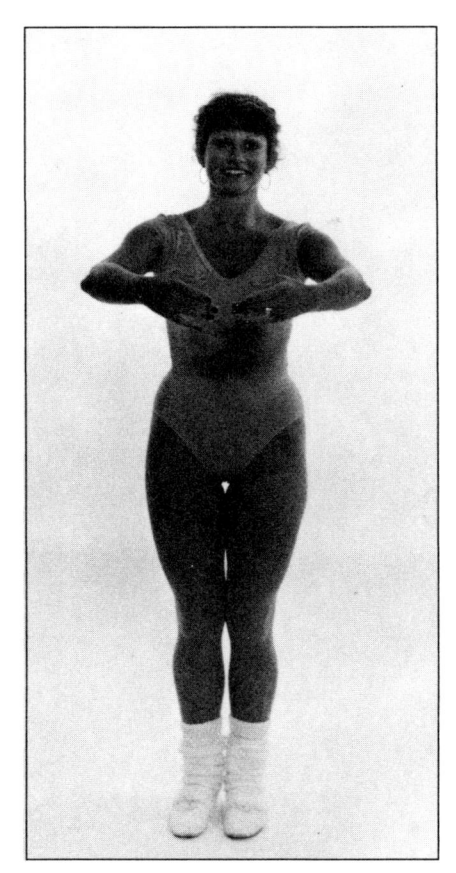

(after 180° turn)

Level I—THE TURN—Step R to R for the first count; turn your body 180° to the R, AST step L on count two; turn your body another 180° to the R and step R on count three. Touch your L foot next to the R to complete the rotation on count four. Your head spots to the R; repeat with your other side.

ALL THAT JAZZ AND MORE... 185

Level I—VARIATION—On count four when your L foot touches, contract your pelvis and accent the contraction with your R arm by giving it a sword-like effect motion inward to your rib cage.

Level II—VARIATION—Substitute a ball change for the last touch movement.

Level II—VARIATION—Incorporate a full head roll while turning. If turning to the R, head drops forward, R, back, L.

Level I—VARIATION—Lunge to the R on the third count instead of stepping to the R and hold on count four.

CHAINÉ TURN

Level I—Similar to the three step turn only keep your momentum going into a series of turns in one direction. Keep your arms close to the fifth position while turning and open to the second position after completion of a turn. (Example: Step R to R on count one with your arms in the second position; pivot 180° to the R again and step L with your arms in the fifth position on count two; pivot 180° to the R again and step R, open your arms to the second position on count three; pivot 180° to the R and step L and continue.) Your head spots forward or to the side. Every turn is approximately one foot in width apart.

ALL THAT JAZZ AND MORE... 187

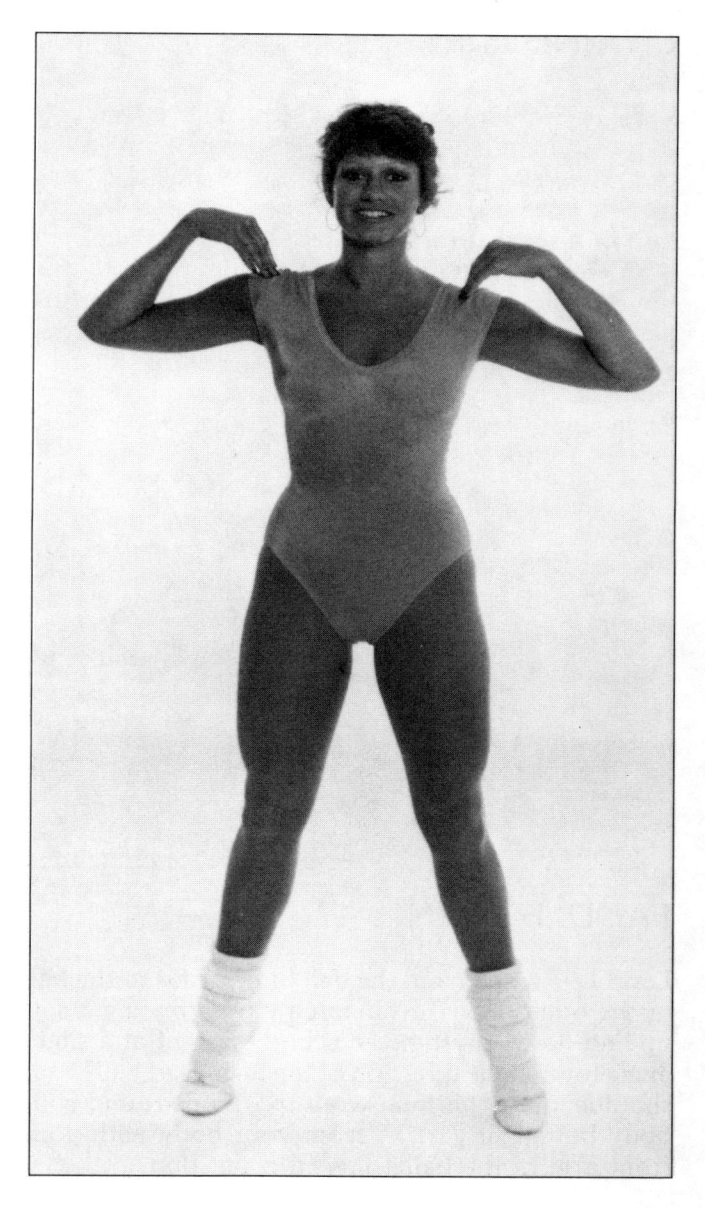

Level I—VARIATION—Touch your hands lightly on your shoulders while turning. This exercise is good for practicing foot movement and spotting.

Level I—VARIATION—On each continuous chaîné turn, change arm positions from first to second to a high fifth.
Note: See Locomotive Chapter for more variations.

Note: Chaînés can be performed two ways: either with straight legs as illustrated or relevé by turning out on each step (high chaînés) or in a plié-relevé position with your feet parallel (low chaînés). A good exercise is to do four consecutive turns high, four low, four high, etc. Always turn on the ball of your foot.

PADDLE TURN

Level I—Switch from the ball of one foot to the ball of the other, AST turning in a circle creating a soft up and down rhythm; your body is bent at a slight angle toward the direction of the turn; lead with your shoulder and arms in a "wrap" position around your body but slightly away from your body with your front arm in the ballet low fifth position.

PENCIL TURN

Level I—Begin in a side lunge position with your arms in the second position. Bring your feet together by placing your extended leg tightly next to your bent leg, AST close your arms to the fifth position and rotate 360° outside (backwards); squeeze your legs together while spotting to the front. This turn is done with the weight on the balls of both feet. End the rotation by bringing your arms out to the second position again.

BARREL TURN

Level II—Same as a pencil turn, only your body is bent forward from your trunk with eye contact toward the audience. Your arms are in the jazz second position creating a windmill effect.

SOUTENU TURN

Level II—From the ballet fifth position with your R foot back, slide your R foot to the side as your L leg bends in a demi-plié. Draw your R foot straight in to the fifth position relevé to the front; AST a turn L 360° on both feet and end with your L foot in front. Your arms come from the second position to the high fifth position to the second position again.

SPIRAL TURN

Level I—In a demi-plié, cross one foot in front of the other; keeping feet in place, rotate 360°; notice that your legs will end up in a switched position.

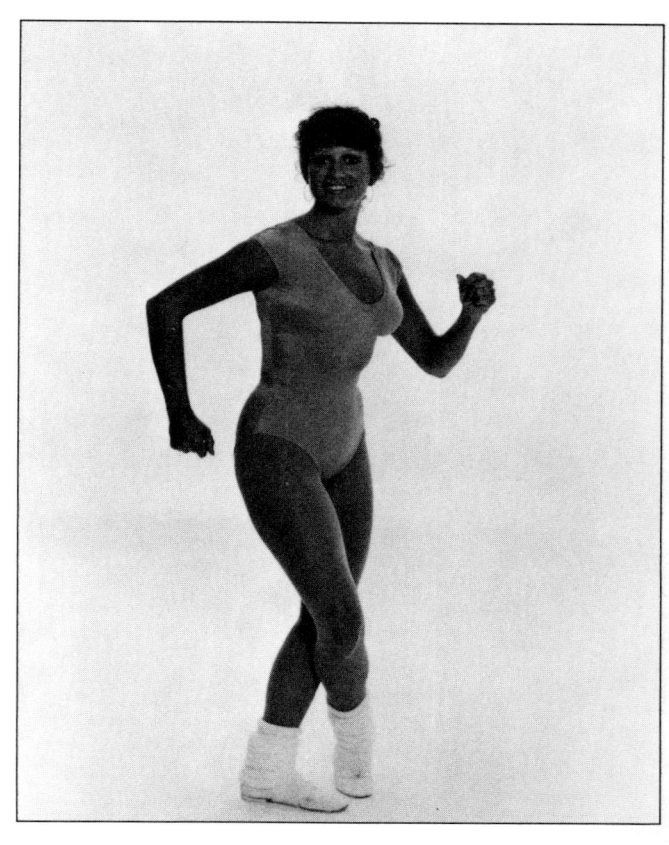

JACKSON TURN

Level II—In a demi-plié, cross your R leg over your L leg bearing most of the weight. As you turn, bring your arms and elbows in toward your body. (The greater the number of turns, the closer your arms come into your body.) This turn is done on both feet while spotting to the front.
Note: Quick spotting and a gradual pull of your arms closer to your body will create a faster turn.

HIP ROLL TURN

Level II—In a demi-plié, cross your R leg behind your L leg AST bring your pelvis forward; keep your feet in place and rotate 360° to the R while your hips make a complete circle to the R, back, L, and front; two hip rolls can be done in one turn.

Level III—VARIATION—Grand plié during the first half of the turn, then spiral up during the first half of the turn, then spiral up during the last half.

DRAG TURN

Level I—Step L to your L side in a small lunge turned out with your arms in the third en avant position. Pivot to the L on your L foot and turn 360° while dragging your R foot next to your L on the side of your R big toe.

OUTSIDE PAS DE BOURRÉE TURN

Level II—This is a three step turn performed ball, ball, flat with your feet in plié-relevé position. Example: In the second jazz position feet with your arms in the second position. Step L to L, simultaneously turning your body 120° to the L. Continue turning 120° to the L and step to the R; complete the 360° turn by crossing your L in front of your R. This can be done by moving back or forward.

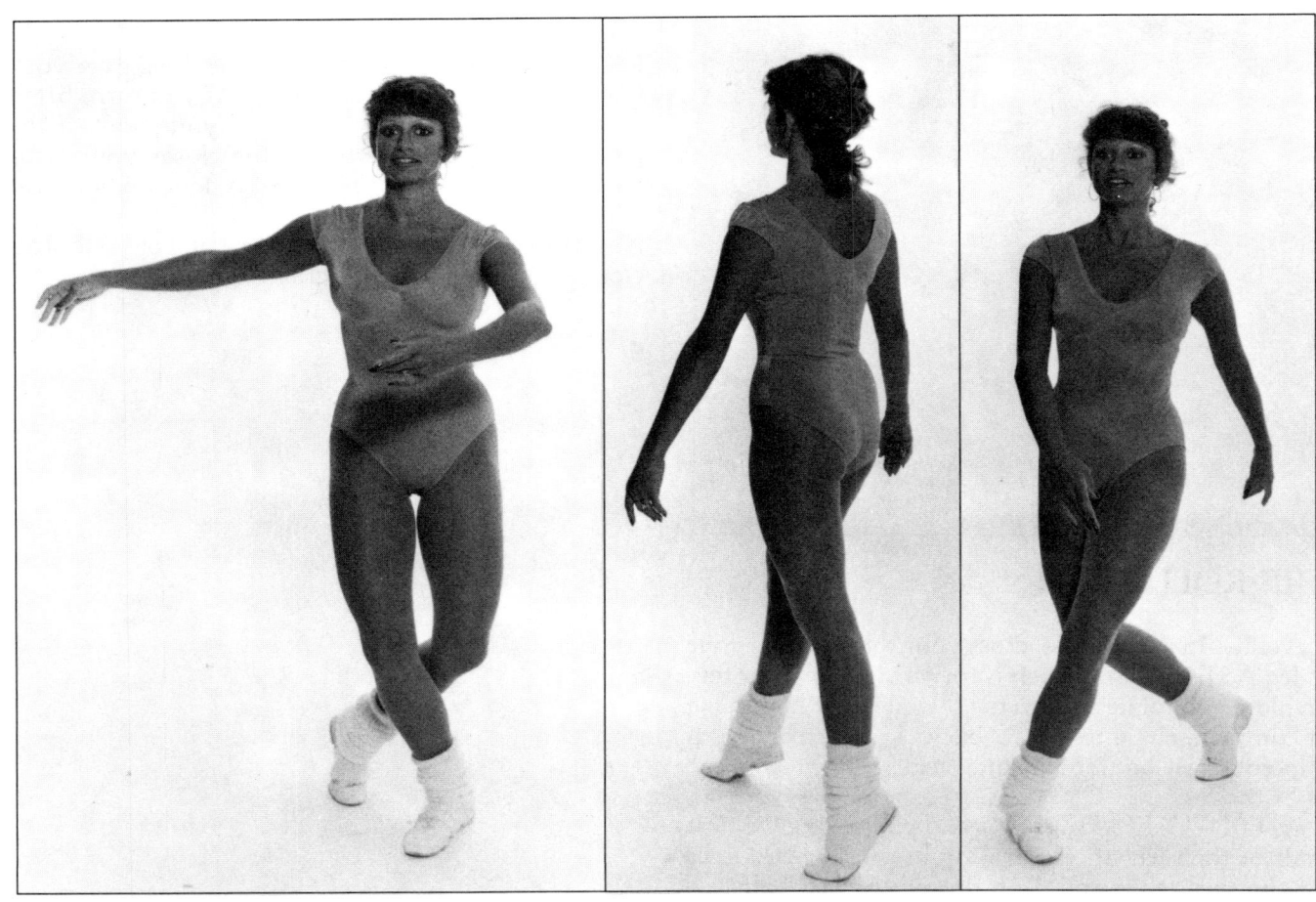

ALL THAT JAZZ AND MORE... 193

CHAINÉ FAN KICK TURN

Level I—PROGRESSION—Perform a series of chaîné turns and a series of fan kicks as described in the chapter on kicks.

Level II—THE TURN—Perform a low chaîné turn L (step L, R). Instead of placing your L foot for the third step, lift your foot into an outward fan kick rotation. If doing a series of turns, place your L foot down after the fan kick, turn 180° to your L and step R; fan your L again as turning 180°.

TURN IN THE AIR

Level II—PROGRESSION—From a jazz first position, demi-plié and jump 90° to the R with your legs straight and your toe pointed; AST your arms come from a ballet first position to a high fifth. Repeat three more times and end facing the front. Then jump 180° twice; 270° three times and finally 360° once. Always land in a demi-plié and spot. Repeat other side.

Level III—THE TURN—Chassé forward; jump with your feet together; jump into the air AST rotate 360° maintaining a straight body with your arms in a high fifth; finally land on your back foot and repeat.

One Footed Turns

LOW JAZZ WALK TURN

Level I—Step with your R foot forward in a low jazz walk position (see Locomotive Chapter). Pivot 360° to the outside (L) with your knee in the forward passé position and your supporting leg in a plié-relevé position. Step L down; walk R and repeat turn spotting front. Reverse.

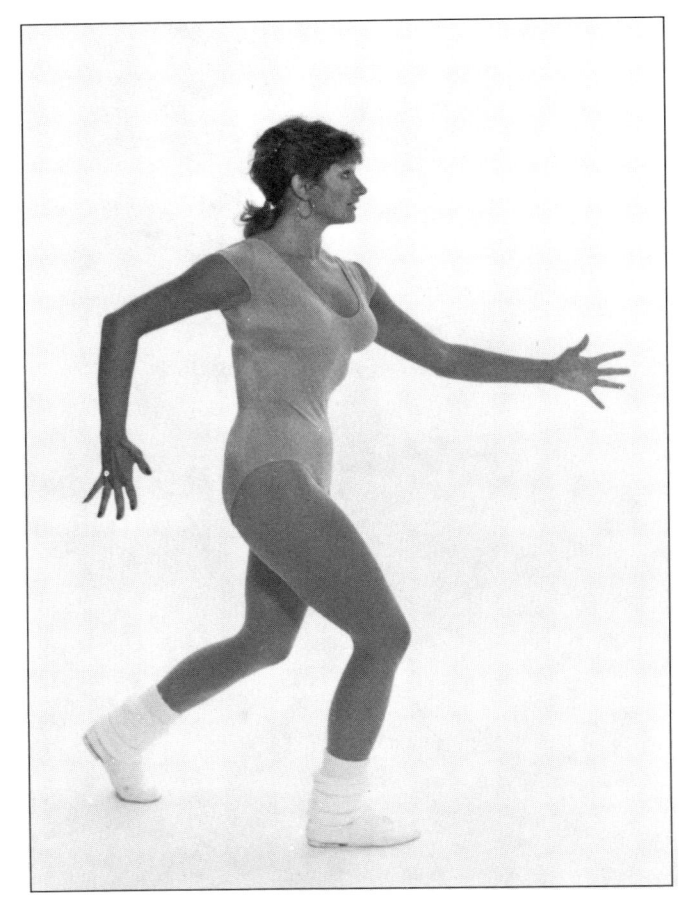

ALL THAT JAZZ AND MORE... 195

LOW OUTSIDE JAZZ TURN

(from a kick ball change)

Level I—PROGRESSION—Small kick across your body with your L foot; place your L foot to the side and change your weight from the ball of your L foot to the ball of your R foot. AST place your arms in the third position; bring your L foot to the forward passé position, AST place your R leg in a plié-relevé with your arms close in the low fifth; hold for two counts; step down to the L in a plié and extend your leg R to the side with your toes pointed and your arms in the second position; repeat with your other side.

Level I—THE TURN—Same as before only instead of holding for two counts, perform a full turn on your R leg to the outside (to the L); repeat with your other side.

Level II—VARIATION—Two full jazz turns instead of one in the same amount of time.

Level II—VARIATION—Perform the turn in a relevé position with your legs straight instead of in a plié-relevé.

Level III—Three or more turns in a plié-relevé position.

Note: If you are performing a single turn and your arm preparation is in the third en avant position, you only need to close your arms from the third position to the fifth position to give yourself the momentum of one turn. At the end of the turn, the opening of your arms to second position assists in stopping you. For two or more turns, prepare your arms in the third position, but open your front arm to the second position before closing in the fifth position. For example, in the jazz turn described before, quickly open your L arm to the second position, then close to the fifth position as you begin turning. You will get more momentum for the number of turns you need. For more than three turns, repeat as described before only gradually bringing your arms closer to your body while you turn in order to shorten your radius. One other pointer—for more than four turns, begin in a deeper demi-plié position and eventually straighten your legs as you turn.

LOW INSIDE JAZZ TURN
(from a kick ball change)

Level I—Same as the outside jazz turn, only the rotation is performed forward (to the R).

Level II—VARIATION—Do the turn with a straight leg on relevé.

PIROUETTE FROM SECOND POSITION

Level II—PROGRESSION—Begin in the ballet fifth position with your R foot back; tendu (see index) to the side with your L foot; plié in the jazz second position with your arms in the third en avant position and bring your L leg to the forward passé, AST relevé on your R leg; with your arms in the close fifth position. Hold for two counts and close in the ballet fifth position with your L foot back. Repeat with your other side.

Level II—THE TURN—Substitute a 360° turn to the L for the hold with your L leg in a forward passé and your supporting leg in a relevé.

Level II—VARIATION—Inside pirouette; rotate inward (to the R) instead of outward. Your arms will have to change on the preparation with your L arm out to the second position and your R arm forward; repeat with your other side.

Level III—VARIATION—Double or more rotations on the turn inward or outward.

Level III—VARIATION—Perform a forward pas debourrée traveling forward; on the last step, demi-plié and perform an outside double pirouette; repeat with your other side.

ALL THAT JAZZ AND MORE... 199

PIROUETTE FROM FOURTH POSITION

Level II—PROGRESSION—Begin in the ballet fifth position with your R foot back, tendu L to the side and place your L leg back in the ballet fourth demi-plié position. With your arms in the third with your arms closing to the fifth position; hold for two counts; close your L foot to the position; repeat with your other side.

Level II—THE TURN—Same as before only perform an outside turn (to the L) instead of holding for two counts. Repeat with your other side (turning to the R).

Level II—VARIATION—Turn an inside pirouette (to the R) instead of an outside pirouette, which means your arms will have to change in the third position with your R arm forward and your L arm in the second position.

Level III—Double or more rotation either inside or outside.

Level III—VARIATION—Perform an inside pirouette and kick out to a second position after rotating 360° or more.

Level III—VARIATION—Perform an outside pirouette and extend leg into a back arabesque (see index) after rotating 360° or more.

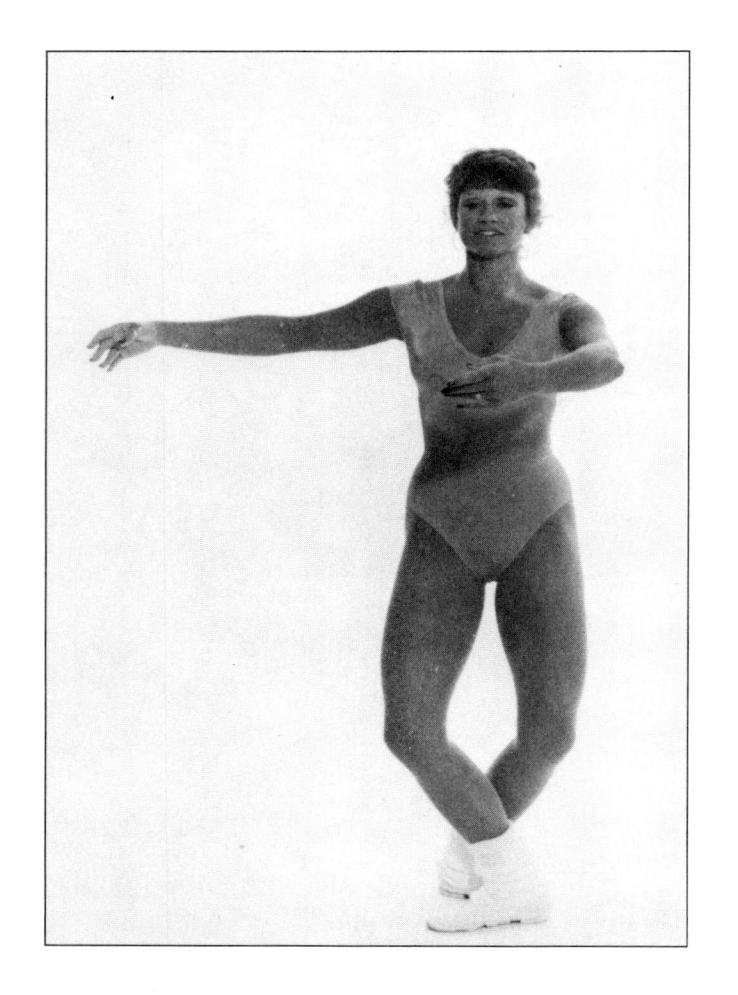

PIROUETTE FROM THE FIFTH POSITION

Level II—Begin in the ballet fifth position with your R foot back; tendu to the side with your L foot and place your L leg in the ballet fifth position; demi-plié with your arms in the third position. Lift your L leg to a sur le cou-de-pied position, (your foot placed at your ankle with your heel in front and your toes in back), AST your supporting foot relevés; hold for two counts; place your L foot behind your R in the ballet fifth position; repeat with your other side.

Level II—Same as before, only perform an outside turn (to the L) instead of holding for two counts. Repeat with your other side (turning to R).

Level III—VARIATION—Turn an inside pirouette by tendu second with your L foot. Plié your L foot front in the fifth position; turn inside (R), lifting your R foot instead of your L; after turning, close your R foot back. Repeat with your other side.

Level III—Double or more inside or outside turns.

PIQUÉ TURN (PI KĀY)

Level I—PROGRESSION—Face to the L in the ballet fifth position with your L foot to the front and your arms in the ballet third position. Point your front foot to the L and quickly step on it in a relevé, AST bring your R foot to the sur le cou-de-pied (see index) position in front of your supporting ankle with your arms in the close fifth position. Hold for one count; come down on your R leg in demi-plié with your L foot extended to the side and slightly lifted off the floor and your arms in the second position. Repeat in a series; try the other side.

Level II—THE TURN—Same as before only instead of holding for one count, turn 360° on your supporting L leg to the outside (to the L). Repeat with your other side.

Level II—VARIATION—Same as before, only place your free R leg in a turned out passé position or in an extended straight position.

Level III—VARIATION—Pique turn in the air. Chassé L, R, L forward; jump from your L leg and perform a 360° turn in the air to the L with your R leg in a sur le cou-de-pied position with your arms in a low or high fifth position. Come down on your R leg in a demi-plié and repeat; try your other side. Note: The series of turns can be executed diagonally, around, or straight across the room.

ARABESQUE TURN

Level II—Turn 360° outward (to the L) on your L supporting foot with your R leg extended backwards in a back arabesque, arm position optional. Repeat with your other side.

ATTITUDE TURN

Level II—Turn 360° outward (to the L) on your L supporting foot with your R leg extended backwards in an attitude. Repeat with your other side.

Level II—VARIATION—Turn outward (to the L) on your L supporting leg with your R leg in a forward attitude and your body slightly contracted forward; repeat with your other side.

FOUETTÉ TURN

A series of turns on your supporting leg, whipping your working leg in a quarter circle while turning.

Level II—PROGRESSION—Begin with your body facing slightly to the R in the ballet fourth position, your L foot to the front. Execute an outside pirouette with your L foot in a sur le cou-de-pied position 360°. Then thrust your working leg energetically forward at a 45° angle across your other leg; AST demi-plié on your supporting leg with your R arm at chest level and your L arm swinging out to the side. Repeat with your other side.

Level III—THE TURN—Swing your working leg and R arm to the second position in the air, rising and turning on the relevé of your supporting foot. Whip your working leg inward, passing your toe quickly from the back to the front of your supporting knee. Swing your rounded arms forcefully together. To continue a series, thrust your working leg forward (across your body at a 45° angle) and descend easily on each turn by a demi-plié on your supporting leg. Open your arms to second position at the termination of each turn.

As you become advanced and learn the techniques of spotting, you will be able to perform an inside, outside and double turn at the same time. Try putting a few turns together and learn to flow from one to another. Some examples include:

1. Two chaîné turns; pas de bourrée; outside pirouette; repeat.
2. Tendu a second position to preparation fourth; outside pirouette; jump into a second position and pirouette again.
3. Front attitude turn; immediately into a multiple of chaîné turns in a square.
4. Outside pas de bourrée turn; use the last step as a preparation and pirouette outside on your straight leg; step forward L, R and reverse.
5. Kick ball change; double inside pirouette; kick your lifted leg out to the second position; cross your lifted leg over your supporting leg; Jackson turn.
6. Kick ball change; outside double jazz turn; step down on your lifted foot and perform an inside jazz turn; ball change outside pirouette immediately into a back arabesque turn.

12 Putting It all Together— Choreography

To choreograph is to create and all of us have unlimited creative potential. So, there's no need to rely on others for choreographic material. You can develop your own. Just as your muscles need time to develop and grow through constant effort, so does the creative consciousness of your mind. How do you begin?

You now have been exposed to the basic steps and techniques in jazz dance. As a novice, try combining the moves you have just learned. Take a few of the steps and put them together (for example, a chassé, chaîné turn, jazz square, pas de bourrée) and then try them in reverse! Add your unlimited imagination and pow!...there's your choreography. If you are choreographing a class combination, keep the beginning routines short and simple so you can work on weight transitions, body directions, and smoothness. For the advanced routines you may want to lengthen the routine, add more difficult movements, and change the rhythm so you're not always on the beat.

Choreographing a dance for a production or a show is a little more difficult. A few pointers that may help you get started include:

1. DEVELOP A THEME—This is one of the easiest tasks of choreography. Some theme examples are: telling a story or idea, a tribute to a musician or a motion picture, centering on a word such as "magic" or "hoedown," or a tribute to a culture. You may just want to create emotions, ideas, images or an atmosphere as your theme. Perhaps the music you select will give you a story or theme. Make sure the theme fits the age group and audience viewing your performance. For example, you would not want to have a very sensuous production for a family audience!

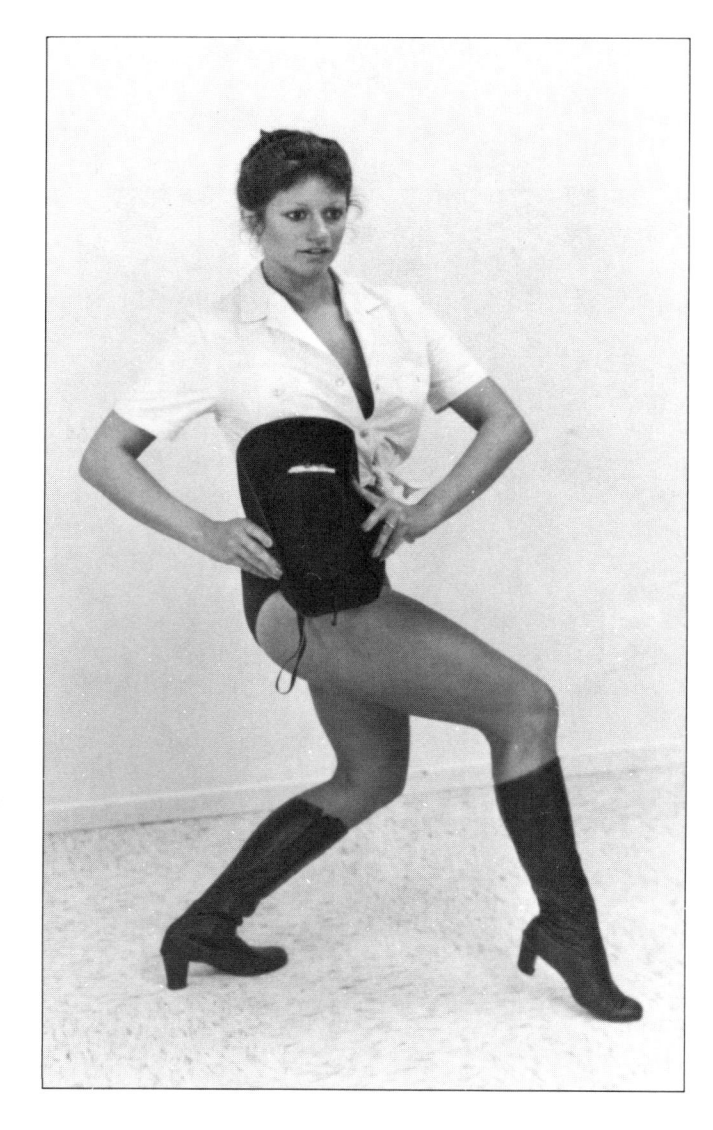

Choreographic Floor Patterns

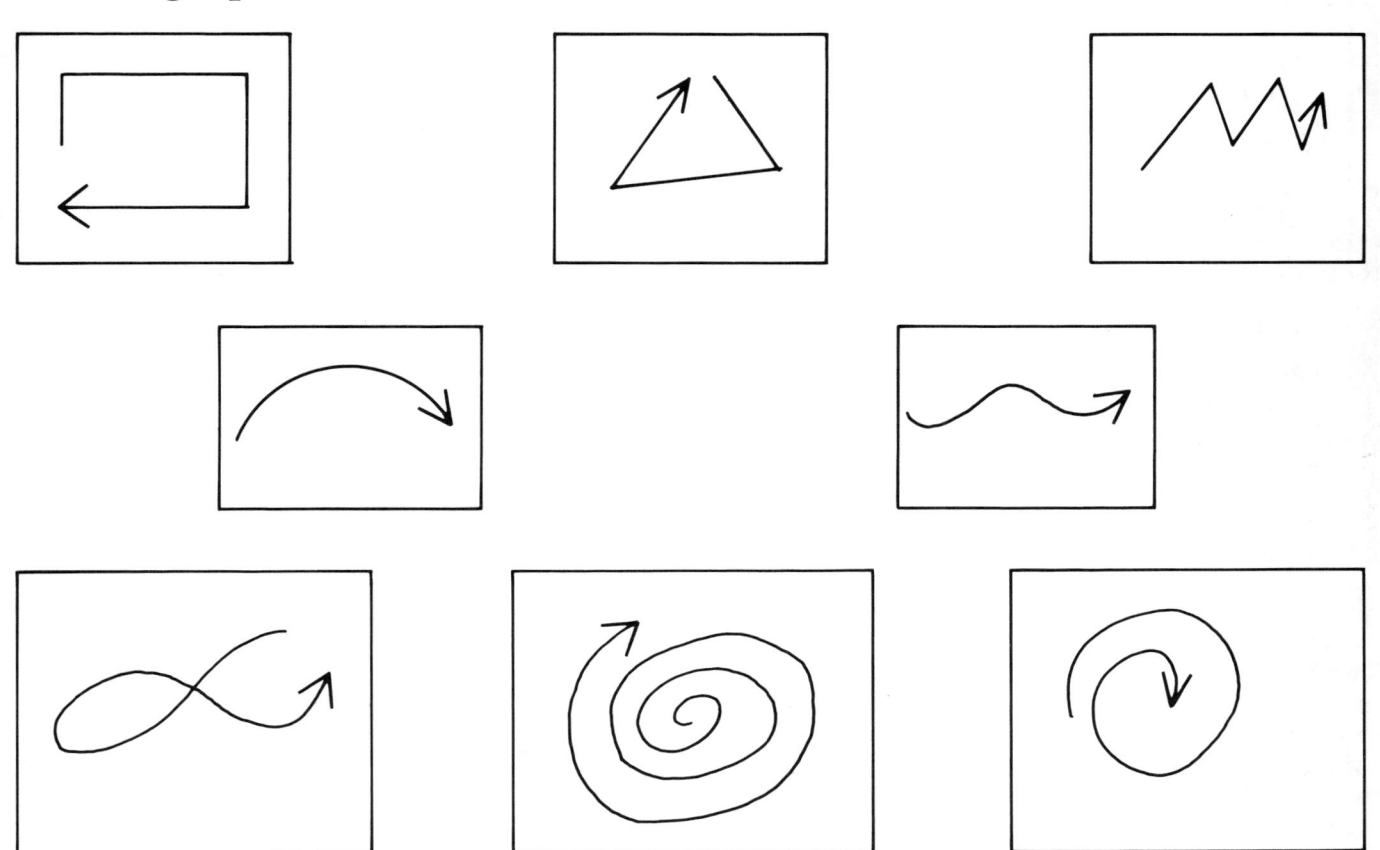

2. FIND YOUR MUSIC—Keep the music consistent with your idea or theme. Try diversifying the style of the music or "age" of the music. You can select music from almost all fields; rock, disco, dixieland, soul, country, African, Latin, jazzed up folk and classics. Just make sure the routine fits the music. A good variation is to try sounds, poems, words or even silence. Remember, you can always make the music exciting with your movements.

Analyze the structure of the music. Develop a chorus where movements can be repeated and you can accent irregularities. Distinguish which part of the music will be for individuals or for groups. Note the changes in times, tempos, beats, phrases and energy. Try composing your own music or use live music. One instrument can make an enormous effect. Currently on the market is a rhythm matrix that produces variable syncopation to fit your needs.

3. DEVELOPING THE MOVEMENTS—Use the steps and movements in this book as a base for your dance. Use the entire floor, all the space you have to work with, and make sure of diversity of floor patterns. Be careful of stage designs. For example, symmetrical "lines" dancing is the easiest and most popular form of dancing, but it can become tedious after awhile.

Always check your choreography. Do you have a balanced routine? Are there:
Rising movements?
Descending movements?
Inward movements?
Outward movements?
Continuous movements?
Abrupt movement?
Directional changes?
Body waves or contractions?
Holds or balances?
Accents?
Gymnastics or mime?

Do not feel it is necessary to include all, but there should be enough variety to complete the picture. Are all transitions smooth especially between turns, jumps and locomotor moves? How is the use of time? (You may not want to always go on the beat.) Did you give resting points or breathing points so the dancers do not sound like a train engine huffing and puffing through the routine? Remember, what will stick in the audience's minds more than anything is the entrances and exits. Is there anything original or exciting about yours? Does the overall dance fit your group's personality and age level? Can you add or take away from the choreographed piece by adding costuming, lighting, or props?

4. IMPROVISATION—Subconscious related improvisation is the best way to create. It means to compose or invent on the spur of the moment. Improvisation is a chance to express and experiment with your own body, with music or rhythm, with space, with concepts, and emotions. Put yourself into a room or studio alone (preferably with the door locked), turn on some music and let your body go. You'll be surprised at your creative ingenuity! Occasionally envision an audience and try to create for them. This procedure is not only a great way to develop your own style of choreography, but also an excellent aid to help you handle the situation while a "blackout" occurs during a performance. Remember, this procedure when done correctly allows your subconscious to operate. It is something all of us should do occasionally to get out of the structured world.

5. PUTTING IT ALL TOGETHER—Don't ever forget to look at the number as a whole, since it is so easy to get wrapped up in just fragments. Title the piece so that you make sure the title adequately reflects the idea of the work. Is the element of time correct for the piece? (A four hour number can be a little long for the audience!) Well rehearsed—sometimes the easiest routine executed perfectly together can be the best routine. And lastly—perform it; the next chapter will show you how.

13 Now Dance It!

Dance, like any art form, is a means of self-expression and communication with the body. It is *performed* for the purpose of entertaining the audience.

Feelings can be communicated more so than body movements. So why not release your inner feelings and enjoy! Unless a dance is performed with feeling, it does nothing for the audience. And if you do not feel the dance yourself, you are missing out on the greatest part of dancing! The inner experience will come to you if you let it. But "how," you say?

One of the most difficult obstacles for jazz dancers especially for a beginning dancer, is to forget their self-consciousness and "let go." As a beginner or even an advanced student, you probably feel some emotions getting in your way; i.e., nervous tension, anxiety, or maybe low self-esteem. How can you get rid of these psychological barriers?

It takes training, a form of mental training that you must develop just as you physically train your body to develop a muscle. It is the same form of training professional athletes go through. Just as an athlete is about to go out to a competition, so must a dancer prepare for a performance. For some, psychological training is more necessary than physical training.

If you are a perfectionist, intimidated by others, overassertive, super sensitive, insecure, overconfident, a nervous wreck or even an "iceberg," your performance may be affected. These types of behavior are all emotional characteristics. Perhaps you are the type of individual who unfairly places psychological pressures on yourself. For example, you may make unjust comparisons between yourself and dancers whose motivations and talents are on a level you can never reach. You make such a comparison simply on performance leaving out all other reasons—health, economics, geographic location, family, etc.

Misdirected emotions, however, often result in psychological pressures on a dancer. In turn, this may result in problems with your physical performance. You should keep in mind that your emotions effect every cell in your body. Your mind and body are intertwined. Don't compromise your capabilities with misplaced emotions.

Pressure can cause anxiety and be manifested as tension. Anxiety is a distraction that can hinder performance, ruin judgment and even make you sick. You may never get over the tension, but you can learn how to channel it to aid in a better performance. Everyone seems to feel that the pressures and self doubts are their own dark secrets, but even good dancers have such problems. They really do. They just know how to handle them. Remember, the biggest anxiety producer is you.

Let's generalize how you can better channel your energies in a more positive way. Self-awareness is the first step towards being in better control of your dancing. Become aware of your body and mind by tuning in to your feelings and emotions. Then put yourself in a relaxed state of mind and body by getting loose and breathing easy. At all times, however, remain focused on the task at hand.

In dancing, concentration is more difficult than in ordinary circumstances, since it is usually done under pressure. The higher the anxiety the shakier the concentration. When you feel anxiety, your worries, doubts, anger, frustration, self consciousness and discouragement tend to crowd your attention. Because your mind pays attention to only one thing at a time, it will tend to push out the things on which you were trying to concentrate. Furthermore, the feelings these emotions engender tend to be more compelling to your imagination than the cool, rational action on which you had intended to focus attention. (Thus, you concentrate best when you are relaxed.)

Concentration collectively refers to the instructions you give yourself in the form of images (of your routine). If you imagine yourself successfully doing your routine, the negative emotions will not have a chance to get in. This action is called mental rehearsal. It involves you imagining yourself making the dance moves. The more vivid and detailed the image, the better your body can understand what it has to do. Mental rehearsal makes psyching a habit—your reactions are automatic (the response you have learned best) and there is no need to think. This is one reason why just watching someone dance well can improve the quality of your own performance.

Perhaps you can recall positive moments when everything seems to click. Probably the major element that you would recall is that you were *totally* involved in what you were doing...unaware of yourself as the doer, aware only of the completed dance.

These high moments have four qualities: 1) you are physically free and unhampered by tension; 2) you are mentally focused (on here and now); 3) you are in harmony with the body and mind; and 4) you are enjoying it—it feels right. This is the state that you want to reach.

Mental rehearsal is not to be confused with wishful thinking or even positive thinking. Wishful thinking is fantasizing about something you hope is coming true but over which you have little control. Positive thinking is telling yourself you can do it. Both are concerned with ends rather than means. With mental rehearsal you are thinking and practicing the mean by which you can give your best performance.

So practice mentally as well as physically. The psychological factors are probably the most important, yet are also the most neglected in our approach to dancing.

Some professional dance troupes have what they call a "green room" before a performance where their sole purpose is to get psyched up for the show. Everyone has their own little way to help them get ready for a production. Some people just need to be by themselves before a show. Whatever it takes, mental preparation is a good idea if you want to perform well and enjoy that meaningful inner experience.

14
ROUTINES

This chapter presents two examples of jazz dance routines from the numerous styles that were listed in the beginning of this book that are influencing jazz today. I would describe these two as a basic beginning jazz routine and an intermediate modern jazz routine. These routines are not written completely for the music selected, since they are not intended for learning use, I selected them to give you a better idea of what choreography is about.

The routines will be described in a clock position with twelve o'clock being the audience, three o'clock meaning stage R, six o'clock meaning backstage and nine o'clock being stage L.

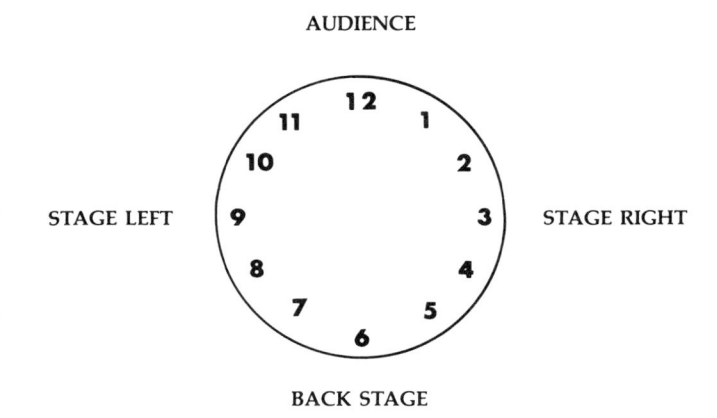

BEGINNING JAZZ ROUTINE

Suggested Music: "On Broadway" by Grover Washington, Jr.

Movements

Counts 1 - 4: Enter stage L with low jazz walks and open palms; walk R, L, R, L.

Counts 5 - 6: Pivot to 12:00 and continue walking R, L.

Counts 7 - 8: Change your walk to a hip walk R, L, accenting the L while stepping into the jazz second position; your arms should be in the second position.

ALL THAT JAZZ AND MORE... 213

Counts 1 - 2: Your shoulder and R knee rotate in and out.

Counts 3 - 4: Lift your R hip into a hip lunge; your L hand is on hip.

Counts 5 - 7: Pas de bourrée (L, R, L) to R; your arms are in the second position.

Count 8: Release your head back; touch your hat with your fingers.

Counts 1 - 3: Chainé R to 3:00.

Counts 4 - 5: Ball change with a shoulder roll; your arms are in the second position.

214 ROUTINES

Count 6: High kick R to 10:00.

Count 7: Step R to R.

Count 8: Step R forward with your hip front; your hand knocks your hat forward.

Counts 1 - 4: Pivot 180° to 6:00 and step L; 180° drag turn L.

Counts 5 - 8: Chassé R to 2:00; your palms come up; chassé L; your arms are in the fourth position.

Counts 1 - 2: Perform a second position jump to the R.

Count 3: Step L foot behind your R foot.

Counts 4 - 5: Spiral 360° turn to the L.

ALL THAT JAZZ AND MORE... 215

Counts 6 - 3: Three traveling kick ball changes (R, R, L) to 11:00; your arms are in the second position with your shoulder leading.

Counts 4 - 6: Use last ball change as a preparation for an outside pirouette on L; step on R foot.

Counts 7 - 8: Outside pirouette on the R foot.

Counts 1 - 2: Cross your L foot over your R foot; slide your R foot; your arms are in a diagonal position.

Counts 3 - 4: Swing your arms in a clock rotation, AST pivot your body to the L and end in a L lunge.

INTERMEDIATE MODERN JAZZ ROUTINE

Suggested Music: "Endless Love" by Diana Ross

Movements

Intro: Begin with your back to the audience on center stage; your L foot crossed over your R with your arms in the ballet first position.

Counts 1 - 16: Raise and lower your arms twice, AST your head looks up to the L side.

Counts 1 - 2: Chainé R to 12:00.

Counts 3 - 4: Piqué R to 12:00 with your L leg extended.

Count 5: Cross L over your R.

Counts 6 - 7: Double chainé R to 3:00; end facing 12:00.

Counts 8 - 2: Jazz palms cross at your wrists and extend upward across your body and downward along the side of your body; slight lean to the R; your L shoulder forward; look to the R.

ALL THAT JAZZ AND MORE... 217

Counts 3 - 4: Pique L to 9:00; end facing 9:00.

Counts 5 - 8: Cross your arms at your wrists, then move them up to a high fifth position crossing your body; then move them down to the first position; wrap your body, AST look to the L; your R foot comes up.

Counts 1 - 3: Outside back attitude turn on the R; your arms come from a low first position to a circle over your head.

Counts 4 + 5 - 6: Walk to 2:00 L, R, L, AST your L arm swings up in front of your body and around a counterclockwise circle; your L arm ends behind your back.

Counts 7 - 8: Step R to 3:00; slide your L foot to the R, AST contract your upper back; both of your arms come under and end in front of your body with your palms flexed.

Counts 1 - 3: Walk backwards L, R, L to 8:00.

218 ROUTINES

Counts 4 - 5: Sweep your R leg back into an arabesque.

Counts 6 - 8: Step backward with your left leg; your arms go behind your body; execute an inward front attitude to the L; cross your hands at your wrists, AST contract your upper body.

Counts + 1 - 2: Stop turn at 10:00 and "reach" your arms from a low fifth position to a second position to a high fifth position. AST relevé in the jazz fourth position.

Counts 3 - 5: Step R to 11:00, AST your arms drop; inward fan kick with a slight lean to the L; your arms are in the second position.

Counts 6 - 8: Cross your L leg over your R; step R to 3:00 facing 3:00; your R arm back.

Counts 1 - 5: One-half outside pirouette turn in a forward passe position on the R. Place your L foot down; two inside pirouettes on your L.

Counts 6 - 2: Bring your R foot down and continue turning into two paddle turns to the L; your arms wrap your body.

Counts 3 - 5: Walk to 7:00 R, L, R.

Counts 6 - 7: Small battement L to 11:00; one-half turn on R; repeat battement to 1:00.

Counts + 8 +: Small runs forward L, R, L.

Counts 1 - 2: High battement R; your arms are in a high "V."

Counts 3 - 4: Bring your R leg to a forward passé; place your R foot down; go to a squat position.

Count 5: Spiral turn L; end facing 1:00.

Counts 6 - 8: Rise to stand watching your R arm come along the side of your body and overhead.

Counts 1 - 4: Body wave.

Counts 5 - 8: Perform L splits with your L hand on the floor for support.

Counts 1 - 2: Cross R over L into a seat spin; your arms cross your chest; end in a swastika.

Counts 3 - 4: Come up to your knees.

Counts 5 - 8: Your arms circle backwards; then cross your chest.

Count 1: Your R foot steps while your L knee is on the ground.

Count 2: One-half turn to the L with your L leg extended forward off the ground.

Counts 3 - 8: Walk off stage alternating your shoulders.

15
S-T-R-E-T-C-H-ABILITY

If I were given the choice of being strong or flexible, I would choose being flexible. It is much easier to do repetitive strength exercises than to have to sustain a stretch for thirty seconds and "grin and bear it." However, a balance of both is your best bet as a dancer.

Flexibility is an absolute necessity in dance. The extended ranges of motion which are vital to high level choreography could be considered a severe problem if they were found in an average person. Did you know muscles can be stretched 150 percent of their normal length?

Why is stretch so important in dance? Well, first it is a means of improving movement and technique. I cannot understand how anyone can try to master a skill in dance without being flexible enough to attain the skill. Let's take for example a grand battement. How can you stand and practice controlling your kicks to your ear when you do not even have the flexibility to get it there in the first place? Increasing flexibility so that the joint can move through a full range of motion with minimum restriction can add to the movement potential of the dancer. Movement is the key factor to success in dancing. Flexibility is essential for complete motion. Thus, greater flexibility can allow you to perform more complex dance skills and add more variety to your routines.

Secondly, stretching is your biggest safeguard against joint and muscle injury. Injuries to the soft tissues of the muscles are the most common and recurring types of injuries to dancers. Also, an injury can be less severe and your recovery time quicker if you are on an effective stretching program.

Besides guarding against injury, another reason for stretching is that it reduces muscle soreness. Muscle soreness can be the result of over exertion, inadequate conditioning, or overconditioning. The muscle soreness that occurs immediately after exercise will subside after short periods of rest. But soreness that persists over a long period of time is of serious concern. This can be a result of spasms in an exercised muscle that has become fatigued and is unable to achieve complete relaxation. Stretching exercises are very effective in preventing such spasms, especially if done *after* a workout.

Incidentally the muscles of the body have a natural tendency to stretch less with age. Observe the stiffness in older people. This is usually due to the changes in the tissue as well as a lower level of activity. You can counteract this process by an effective stretching program.

Therefore, the combination of greater extension, easier movements, better movement potential and less susceptibility to injury and soreness should be enough to convince you that stretching can lead to a better dance performance.

When should you stretch? Stretching exercises should be done both before and after a class or a performance to warm up your muscles. You should be extra careful to stretch slowly and properly *before* a workout since the tissue temperatures in your extremities are relatively low at this time. Cold muscles and tendons are less stretchable and more vulnerable to accidental injury through overzealous stretching. Proper stretching before jazz dancing, however, can prevent the tears and pulls that can result from the sudden and sometimes extreme movements involved in jazz dancing.

There are two basic ways of stretching: ballistically and statically. Stretching ballistically involves bouncing type movements and should be avoided in every situation. A muscle being stretched has a tendency to contract. The faster and harder you stretch a muscle, the faster and harder it contracts in opposition to the stretch. So you can see that ballistic stretches are self-defeating. Stretching statically is the best method. You should perform each flexibility exercise by proceeding to the position desired (but only to the point of tightness) and holding that position. This coaxes the muscle structure to relax. (A slight pain and a burning sensation is normal.) As a result, no strain is put on the joint area and the muscle groups stay flexible for a much longer time. Proper breathing and a relaxed state of mind are helpful in stretching. Inhaling when reaching and exhaling when sustaining the desired position is recommended. Avoid forcing the static stretch by going beyond the normal range so that pain is elicited. Some individuals feel that such pain will bring additional flexibility. Yet, just the opposite occurs. The pain signals the brain that a muscle pull is occurring. The body overreacts and contracts that particular muscle group in an effort to stop further muscle pull. As a result, greater tightness occurs rather than greater flexibility.

So, remember, when a muscle is jerked into extension it will "fight back" and shorten. When a muscle is stretched slowly and then held in that position, it relaxes and lengthens. Reach into the stretch easily and hold; do not tug or pull. A relaxed, lengthened muscle is more efficient, less prone to injury, and recovers sooner from the stresses involved in dancing.

During the first few weeks of your stretching program, you should hold all stretches ten to fifteen seconds. Then gradually increase to forty-five to sixty seconds after several weeks have elapsed. Always release your body very slowly after holding a sustained position. The exercises should be done daily to get the most benefit. A good flexibility program involves all the major muscle groups. The following is a list of exercises for your own personal stretching routine that can be done daily. (For variations, see the Floor Exercise Technique Chapter.) Also included are sample partner stretching exercises. Partner exercises are one of the best types of stretching because they allow you to completely relax while undertaking each exercise.

A SAMPLE PERSONAL PROGRAM

Neck Flexibility

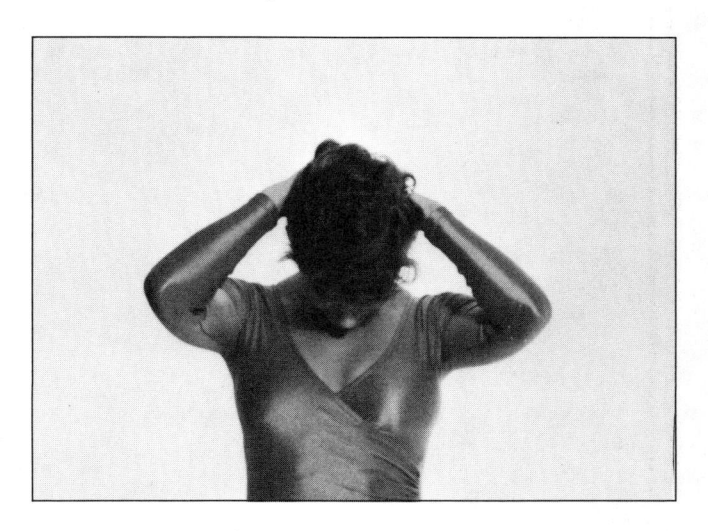

Shoulder Flexibility

Wrist Flexibility

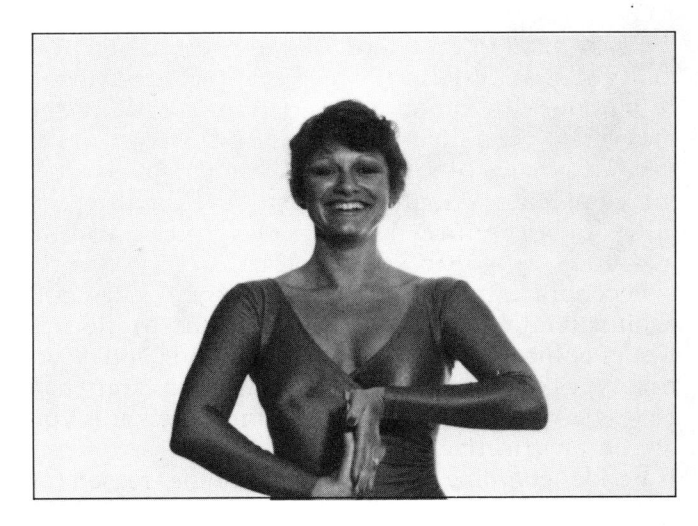

Chest and Upper Back

Lower Back

Abdominals

Side

Hamstrings

ALL THAT JAZZ AND MORE... 227

Hips and Buttocks

Quadriceps and Ankles

228 S-T-R-E-T-C-H-ABILITY

PARTNER PROGRAM

Shoulder

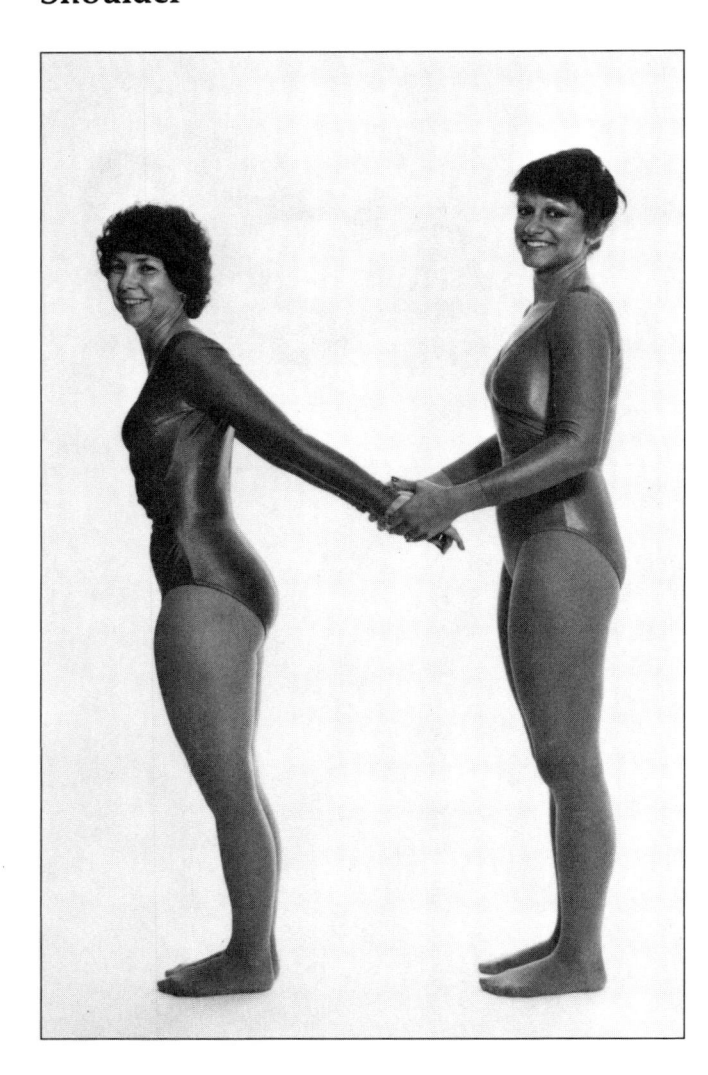

Upper Back

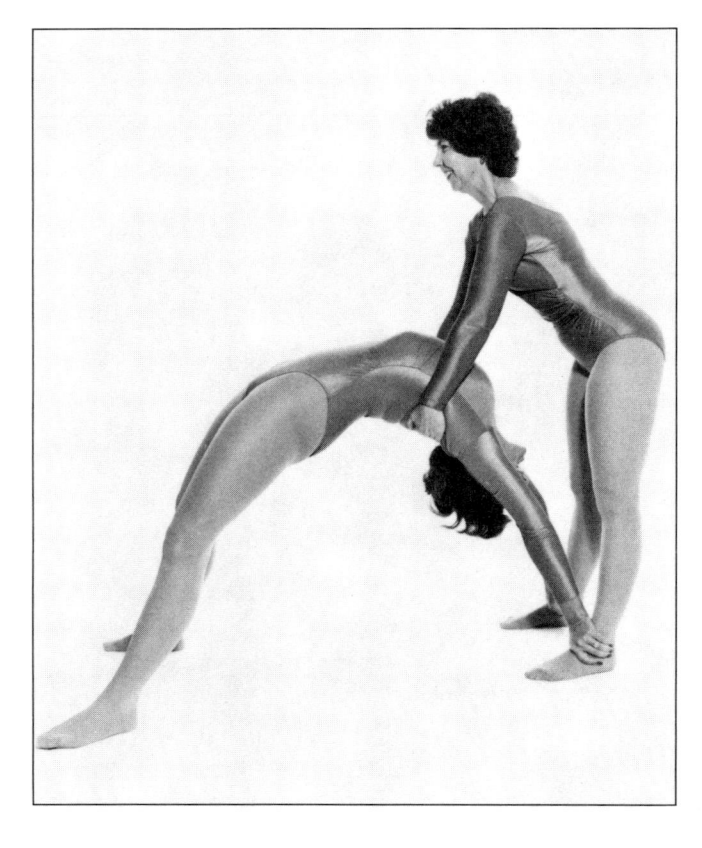

Upper and Lower Back, Chest, and Abdominals

Groin

230 S-T-R-E-T-C-H-ABILITY

Quadriceps (one leg is in a "hurdle" position)

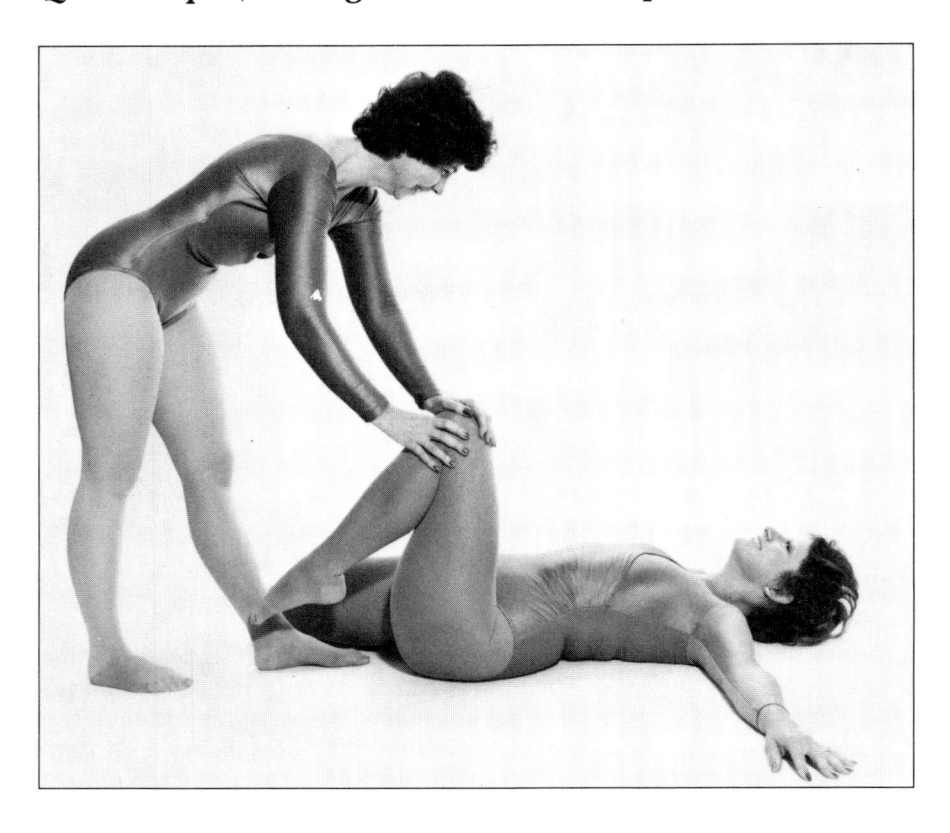

Hamstrings
(Pull partner through)

Calves and Ankles
(Keep legs slightly bent)

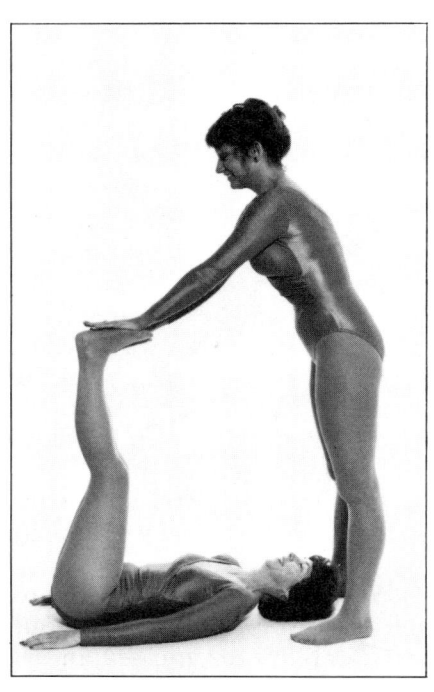

16 The Dancer As an Athlete

It would interest me to review research data on former dancers (and gymnasts) in their latter years to see how healthy their bodies are. I'm sure there are many suffering from chronic pain due to inaccurate advice and inadequate training. Because of the many wonderfully talented and permanently injured or very abused former dancers I have encountered in my travels, I was compelled to write this chapter. Why is it dancers who are so dependent on their bodies abuse them so much? After many inquiries, I discovered that it basically boiled down to two reasons; lack of knowledge and lack of self-responsibility. This chapter very briefly covers both of these areas. I urge you to further your readings in any of the following areas that are of interest to you.

Being involved as a student and teacher in both dance and athletics, I observed much similarity between both fields. It is apparent that as well as being accomplished artists, dancers are superb athletes. Both endeavors require enormous energy by the participants. This is why student dancers and dance teachers must do everything in their power to take care of their bodies. Fortunately, it is not that difficult.

Just as an athlete can benefit from some good solid dance training for body awareness, coordination and suppleness in their sport, dancers can also benefit from proper conditioning, nutritional awareness, injury prevention and treatment, cardiovascular training and relaxation techniques.

Thus, the areas you may want to check yourself on for a higher level of wellness and performance are:

1.) *Self-Responsibility.* This is probably the most important area on this list. Without an active sense of accountability for yourself and your condition, you will not have the necessary motivation to lead a better lifestyle. The greatest cause of poor health in dancers is that most of them neglect themselves or leave the maintenance of their health to others. As a dancer, your body is your instrument, so you must take care of it—no one else will.

2.) *Balanced Strength and Flexibility Program.* It is widely known that one of the nation's major health problems is lower back pain and lower back injuries. In most instances these back ailments are the result of postural misalignment. Such ailments are also caused by a lack of adequate strength in the muscles surrounding the skeletal joints of the lower back and by an imbalance in the strength level between the antagonistic muscle groups of the lower back and abdominal region. In the latter case, the muscles of the lower back and the abdominal area should be approximately equal in strength. When the abdominal muscles increase in strength without a corresponding increase in strength by the lower back muscles, lower back discomfort will result.

The key to minimizing or totally preventing lower back problems is to engage in a properly developed muscular fitness (strength) program. While almost all dancers readily recognize the importance of flexibility and take steps to ensure that the musculature surrounding their joints is supple (and thereby flexible), far fewer dancers accept the fact that they must develop adequate levels of strength if they are to safely sustain their performance levels. If you increase the strength of the musculature surrounding a joint, you decrease the likelihood that joint will ever suffer an injury. Remember, an ounce of prevention is worth a pound of cure. How foolish it would be for you to be sidelined from an activity you love (jazz dancing) because of an injury that might have been prevented.

3.) *Cardiovascular Exercise.* Depending upon their personal programs, some dancers do not receive sufficient aerobic benefits from their dancing workouts. Because of the "stop and go" process of their dance workouts, their cardiovascular systems are not stressed to a point where improvement occurs. Since a healthy heart is at the core of a physically fit lifestyle, it would be advantageous for almost all dancers to engage in an aerobic-type exercise in addition to their dancing. Examples of activities that will develop your cardiovascular system include swimming, aerobic dancing, jogging, cycling, cross country skiing and rowing. It is suggested that an aerobic activity be performed for fifteen minutes continuously at least three times a week. If you select aerobic dancing as your developmental cardiovascular activity, you should be aware that even though quite a few jazz movements are used in aerobic dancing, they are usually danced without control. The main purpose of the movements in aerobic dancing is to get the heart rate going. Aerobic dancing is an excellent activity for a jazz dancer just to "let go" and "have fun" as long as the dancer can resume control of her movements at any time. You should remember before engaging in any aerobic activity to take your pulse and check the charts on your minimum and maximum heart rates for the activity. Aerobic exercise, combined with a diet low in fat and no smoking, is the best way to take care of your cardiovascular system.

4.) *Diet and Nutrition.* Diet and proper nutrition can play a vital role in your performance. Despite the controversy surrounding dieting, most authorities agree on the following common denominators in a proper diet:

1. Eat fruits and vegetables daily.
2. Eat high fiber such as whole grains daily.
3. For protein sources, stay with lean products such as poultry, fish, beans, and low-fat milk.
4. Avoid fats and refined sugar as much as possible.
5. Do not be "afraid" of carbohydrates.

As a dancer, it would be to your advantage to eat six small meals a day. Do not skip meals or change your diet prior to a performance (i.e. carbohydrate load). Watch your fat intake as much as your calorie intake. The "inside" of your body is as important as the outside. Consult experts to determine your ideal body fat percentage. The recommended levels are 10% or less for men and less than 20% for women. So the next time you have a desire for sweets, eat whole wheat or vegetable products instead of junk food. If you eat a balanced diet with sufficient amounts of each of the four basic food groups, you do not need to ingest any food or vitamin supplements whatsoever. There have been numerous studies that have conclusively documented the fact that for a person who eats a balanced diet, such supplements are a total waste of money. It also has been widely documented that drugs, alcohol and caffeine are counterproductive to the health of a dancer (and everyone else also).

5.) *Mental Conditioning.* Training and performing involve more than the physical aspects of the activity. They also require adherence to the "mental" side of dancing. Read the chapter "Now Dance It" to learn how to better cope with performing pressures. By controlling your mind (which takes practice) you can gain absolute control over your body. You can learn how to make proper use of pure emotional energy. You can thus discover that mental training is practice in the art of living—a way of life.

Enjoyment rather than compulsive achievement is the best principal of training. Ninety-eight percent of your dance life is spent training, practicing and rehearsing. So, learn to enjoy the process of training itself.

To "psyche" is to be worry free, calm and alert and to get the most out of the dancing physically, mentally and emotionally.

Learn how to both tolerate and give criticism. Learn how to set and accomplish short and long term goals. The effort of visualization—mentally practicing what you want to achieve—is an effective aid to competition and preparation. Imagine with pictures, feelings and words the roles you want to play.

It's interesting how "hyper" dance students and teachers can get. As you develop your energy to a certain level, stay in control of it. If you are unable to relax outside dancing, learn deep relaxation techniques. You may even want to take courses in stress management if controlling stress is a problem. Inner peace is a lofty goal for all dancers.

6.) *Stay active if you decide to finish your dancing career.* You might as well recognize that lack of exercise can lead to premature bodily aging. The results can be manifested by infirmity, feebleness, frailness and low energy levels. If you end your dancing career, keep dance or some other athletic activity as a recreational hobby. Some of the physiological benefits of staying active are low blood pressure, reduced body fat levels and a better support for your skeletal structure. It can also give you greater self-confidence and an increased ability to manage stress.

In conclusion, the right mental, emotional and physical approach to yourself will radiate a positive, relaxed, confident attitude and body.

17 FOR TEACHERS ONLY

If you are a teacher of jazz dance, you are in a wonderful occupation. You have a job of helping others in a very creative and exciting world of entertainment where you will meet all types of wonderful people while challenging yourself physically and mentally.

The following questions are frequently asked by teachers like yourself. Remember, you are never alone!

Q. How can I motivate my students?

A. Students work more willingly for a teacher they like. Take pains to humanize yourself to students by facts about your interests, family, anecdotes, etc. Friendliness always (but familiarity, never!)

Enthusiasm or lethargy can be contagious. The teacher's own enthusiasm for dance and the day's procedures is essential to any well-motivated class.

Teachers should never strive to be comedians, but a smile or a laugh never hurt anyone. The class that laughs together works together.

Be aware of your own voice and eye contact. Change tone and pitch to maintain interest. Use appropriate gestures in moderation.

Everytime you begin class, try giving the students a word, phrase, or idea to concentrate on.

Do not let students sit in class or socialize during class. You can either teach them respect or tell them they can drop when you do! Try using students to help with attendance, phone calls, paperwork, or cleaning the studio.

Maintain a good working environment; proper temperature, light and ventilation. Constant neatness bespeaks orderliness and efficiency. Use inspirational posters or bulletin boards of worthwhile ideas.

Q. My dance background is limited. Is it necessary that I demonstrate every movement to my students?

A. There are two types of teachers, the action-oriented and the analytical. In the chapter "Now Dance It," I mentioned briefly about the advantage of students who learn through watching (i.e., automatic reaction and more vivid mental images). I personally have never studied under anyone who could not perform what they were instructing. I feel it would be to your advantage to train as much as possible yourself. However, there are those who, because of physical and training limitations, have taught successfully by verbal explanation. For those teachers I recommend that you enforce "mental images" by encouraging students to observe performances, films, television productions and books. Do not be afraid to single out a few of your best students to demonstrate. This will help instill a feeling of accomplishment and pride in them.

Lastly, if you do not have an extensive dance background, do not feel intimidated. Instead, grasp all you can and pass it on to your students. Give them direction to further enrich their studies and enjoy every day of giving.

Q. I am a small college physical education instructor and would love to begin a dance program in my school. Could you give me some guidelines?

A. More and more jazz dance classes are being offered in the school systems and I think that is wonderful! In order for us to keep jazz dance at a high standard, here are some guidelines:

1. *You must be qualified.* A major in dance education combined with professional studio instruction is probably your best preparation. However, if you did not have the physical education background, I would recommend some studies in exercise science. A good idea is to attend a dance workshop where you can self assess your capabilities to determine if you are qualified.

2. *Present a tally of student interest and a report of the values of offering a dance program to the administration.* The report should illustrate the many valuable contributions of dance education. You may want to include not only its physical benefits, but its theatrical, social, artistic, recreational, therapeutic, aesthetic, and individual benefits as well.

3. *Plan out the financial backing, facility and personnel to help.* By not taking these three into consideration for the future, your successful dance program could come to a screaming halt. Most of your expenses will come from performing (costumes, props, lighting) and hiring qualified personnel. Do not sacrifice your body to a concrete or extremely slippery floor for lack of another facility.

Q. I teach in the school system where I am alotted one hour per activity class with fifteen minutes going to dress time. How can I successfully teach dance in forty-five minutes?

A. Talk to your administration to lengthen it to one and one-half hours! I will assume you have already tried that and since something is better than nothing, here are some suggestions.

Try spending twenty minutes on exercise technique, five minutes on turns, ten minutes on locomotive movement and the remainder on combinations or routines. The movements you use in the exercise and locomotor section can be used in the combinations. A very useful approach would be to concentrate on one technique a week (i.e., turns, walks, leaps, spotting) and make it the execution priority for each class held during that week.

Q. My facility is limited. How can I teach different ability levels in one class?

A. A very good question and probably one of the hardest to answer. Unfortunately, due to economic conditions, many studios and schools are faced with a limited amount of time and thus, must resort to combining classes.

Your best solution would be to keep the advanced classes small by enlarging the beginning level classes. At the beginning stage, students are experiencing and experimenting with their bodies for the first time and do not need as much individual attention. In fact, in larger classes, the novice may feel less inhibited as he/she can get "lost in the crowd."

Try making the intermediate level a "technique only" class and hold auditions for the more advanced levels (the performing class).

Q. How can I grade my students on a creative art?

A. Identify specific objectives for students to reach. One idea would be to grade more by execution of specific techniques skills rather than by the student's natural or unnatural rhythm. Avoid grading beginning students on choreography as they must learn their technique first and their creative use of dance movements will be limited. Try compiling a syllabus which lists levels of specific dance techniques the students must master before advancing.

Q. At what age should you learn jazz?

A. Any age! Because of the natural body positions, there would not be as much danger to the body as other dance forms such as ballet. I know three year olds who just love it! Obviously, you must be aware of what types of movements to teach younger and older students. I would not advise teaching sensuous jazz movements to a six year old! But younger students need rhythm and jazz dancing is a great way to expose it to them.

Q. Which is the best teaching method for my class—records, tapes, musicians, or no music at all?

A. This is a matter of personal preference. Some teachers use musicians or no music (finger clicking and counting) because they want to stop and correct frequently. Having a drummer, bongo player or pianist can be an advantage providing they play to the rhythm you desire and keep an inspired melody. Others prefer taped music to keep the movement going so that a good warm-up of the body occurs. The most economical method is to use phonograph records. I prefer records as I like to change my music frequently to keep it updated.

Q. How can I popularize and expand my program?

A. The best exposure and publicity for your program is to start a performing dance group. This is a great way to get community support and is the least expensive type of publicity. It is also a chance for your dancers to get more involved with the program. There are various dance competitions they can enter to give them goals to strive for. But, be aware of the expense of traveling, costumes, and music before embarking on this project.

Q. I live in an isolated town and could use some new ideas for choreography and instruction. Where should I go?

A. Besides reading literature on the subject, there are numerous films distributed by dance suppliers. Another idea is to hire master teachers to teach at your studio. Of course, dance conventions and caravans are extremely beneficial, but be selective. There are many privately operated conventions and caravans that care charging enormous sums of money for less than qualified instruction. However, it is one of the best means of meeting others in your field and sharing ideas. Camps that last one or more weeks are also a great way to learn as there is more time for extensive training. Again, I stress, inquire into them first and consult people who have attended previously. I have taught at numerous camps myself and have sometimes observed the staff setting very bad examples and have seen unfair student-teacher ratios. I do not want to discourage camps as they can be extremely profitable; just be sure the staff is qualified!

Q. Some of my students have danced and outgrown my teaching. Where do they go from here?

A. It takes an unselfish and wise teacher to ask that question. If the student is quite good and desires to continue to a dancing career, encourage him/her to study at the nearest professional studio. It would be an asset to inform him/her what a dancing career involves (possible change in geographic location, financial pressures, etc.). If the student desires to dance for recreational purposes, have him/her assist in the group's choreography. One can always "grow" in the area of choreography and instruction, right?

Suggested Readings

Ardell, Donald B.: *High Level Wellness*; Rodale Press: Emmaus, PA; 1977.

Arnheim, Daniel D.: *Dance Injuries—Their Prevention and Care*; C. V. Mosby Co.: St. Louis, MO; 1975.

Audy, Robert: *Jazz Dancing*; Vintage Books: New York, NY; 1978.

Baily, Convert: *Fit or Fat*; Houghton Mifflin Co.: Boston, MA; 1978.

Beaulieu, John E.: *Stretching For All Sports*; The Athletic Press; Pasadena, CA; 1980.

Cayou, Dolores Kirton: *Modern Jazz Dance*; Mayfield Publishing Co.: Palo Alto, CA; 1971.

Dance Masters of America, Inc.: *Jazz Syllabus*; Copyright 1976 by Dance Masters of America, Inc.

Dow, Allen: *Jazz Dancing*; Vintage Books: New York, NY; 1978.

Fallon, Dennis D. and Kuchermeister, Sue Ann: *The Art of Ballroom Dance*; Burgess Publishing Company: Minneapolis, MN; 1977.

Fonda, Jane: *Jane Fonda's Workout Book*; Simon & Shuster: New York, NY; 1981.

Furst, Clara and Rockefeller, Mildred: *The Effective Dance Programs in Physical Education*; Parker Publishing Co.: West Nyack, NY: 1981.

Giordano, Gus: *American Jazz Dance*; Edited by Gus Giordano; Orion Publishing House: Evanston, Ill., 1966.

Hammond, Sandra Noel: *Ballet Basics*; Mayfield Publishing Co.: Palo Alto, CA; 1974.

Jacob, Ellen: *Dancing*; Addison-Wesley Publishing Co.: 1981.

Hatchett, Frank: *Jazz Class*; Statler Records, Inc.: New York, NY.

Jones, Susan J., Ph.D.: *Warming Up For Fitness*; "Let's Live" Magazine, October Issue, Oxford Industries, Inc.: Los Angeles, CA; 1982.

Kirstein, Lincoln and Sturart, Muriel: *The Classic Ballet*; Alfred A. Knopf: New York, NY; 1980.

Murray, Ruth L., Editor: *Designs for Dance*; Dance Division of AAPHERD; Reston, VA; 1968.

Penrod, James and Plastins, Janice: *The Dancer Prepares*; Mayfield Publishing Co.: Palo Alto, CA; 1970.

Peterson, James A., Ph.D., Editor, 2nd Edition: *Conditioning for a Purpose*; Leisure Press: West Point, NY; 1983.

Reynolds, Nancy, Editor and Peckolick, Joan, Designer: *The Dance Catalog*; Harmony Books: New York, NY; 1979.

Schmid, Andrea Bodo and Drury, Bannche Jessen: *Gymnastics for Women*; Mayfield Publishing Co.: Palo Alto, CA; 4th edition, 1977.

Stearns, Marshall and Stearns, Jean: *Jazz Dance*; Shirmer Books: New York, NY; 1979.

Steinberg, Cobbett, Editor: *The Dance Anthology*; New American Library: New York, NY; 1980.

Stodelle, Ernestine: *The Dance Technique of Doris Humphrey*; Princeton Book Co.: Princeton, NJ; 1978.

Traguth, Fred: *Modern Jazz Dance*; Dance Motion Press: New York, NY; 1978.

Tutko, Thomas, Ph.D. and Tosi, Umberto: *Sports Psyching*; J. P. Tarcher, Inc.: Los Angeles, CA; 1976.

Unitas, John and Dintiman, George: *Improving Health and Performance in the Athlete*; Prentice-Hall, Inc.: Englewood Cliffs, NJ; 1979.

Vincent, L. M.: *The Dancer's Book of Health*; Sheed Andrew and McMeel, Inc.: Kansas City, MO; 6th printing; 1982.

Wettstone, Eugene, Editor: *Gymnastics Safety Manual*; Pennsylvania State University Press: State College, PA; 1978.

Wydro, Kenneth: *The Luigi Jazz Dance Technique*; Doubleday and Co., Inc.: Garden City, NY; 1981.

INDEX

A
Adage 11
Afro jazz walk 130
Age to dance 235
Arabesque—defined 37
Arabesque turn 203
Arm control (turns) 180
Arm positions—jazz 22
Arm positions—ballet 26
AST 40
Attire for dancing 14
Attitude—defined 38
Attitude swings 122
Attitude turn 204
Attitude twist walk 138

B
Back fall 172
Back hip roll walk 131
Ball change 145
Barre 13
Barrel turn 189
Barrel turn jump 164
Basic jazz steps 16
Basic walk 127
Battement—grand 108
Body alignment 39
Body arch 35
Body roll 36
Bounce walk 133
Breathing 14

C
Camel walk 141
Cardiovascular conditioning 232
Career in Dance 235
Center (dancer's control) 39
Center floor exercises 39
Chaîné 186
Chaîné fan kick turn 193
Chaîné leaps 166
Character walks 132
Chassé—jazz 148
Chassé—ballet 148
Choreography 206
Chugs 149
Class format 13, 234, 235
Combinations 179
Conditioning 231
Contemporary Dances 11
Contraction 36
Conventions, caravans, camps 235
Crossover walks 137
Cross touch walks 136
Cuban walk 142

D
Dance Program 233
Demi-plié 29
Développé 32
Développé stretch 112
Diet 232
Drag 37

238 INDEX

Drag turn 192
Drag walk 131

E
Exercise technique—importance of 39

F
Fan kicks 124
Feelings 210
Flexibility 223
Floor exercises 58
Foot positions—ballet 18
Foot positions—jazz 16
Fouetté battement 164
Fouetté turn 205
Four corners walk 143
French twist walk 138
Front fall 169

G
Glissade—jazz 147
Glissade—ballet 147
Grading 235
Grand plié 29
Grapevine 150
Gymnastics 178

H
Hand positions—jazz 20
Hinge 34
Hip lift walk 140
Hip roll turn 191
Hip walk backward 129
Hip walk forward 128
Hitchkick 125

I
Improvisation 208
Isolations—Head 90
    Shoulders 96
    Arms 98
    Ribs 100
    Hips 104
    Knees 106
    Feet 107
    With walks 127

J
Jackknife jump 162
Jackson turn 191
Jazz in the 80's 11
Jazz run 144
Jazz shoot 151
Jazz split 38
Jazz split slide 174
Jazz square 151
Jazz walks 127
Jumps 56, 158

K
Kick ball change 146
Knee rolls 176

L
Layovers 115
Leaps 165
Levels I - III—defined 14
Lindy 151
Locomotive movement 126
Low back protection 58, 231
Low jazz turn—inside 197
                outside 196
Low jazz walk 130
Low jazz walk turn 194
Lunges 33

M
Mental conditioning 210, 232
Mirror walk 139
Modern dance 11
Motivation 233
Music 207, 235

N
New Yorker 156
Nutrition 232

O
One-footed turns 194
One-half turn 182
Outside pas de bourrée turn 192

P
Paddle turn 188
Pas de bourrée 151
Pas de bourrée turning 151
Pas de bourrée jumping 151
Passé 31
Passé walk back 137
Pelvic Tilt 59
Pencil turn 188
Performing 210
Piqué turn 202
Pirouettes 198
Plié 29, 50
Plié-relevé position 30
Popularity of jazz 11
Port de bras 52
Positive thinking 210
Posture 39
Professional students 235
Publicizing Dance Programs 235

R
Relevé 30
Right angle jump 162
Routines 211

S

School dance programs	233
Second position leap	166
Self-responsibility	231
Shoulder roll	173
Shuffle	155
Side fall	171
Side walk	139
Sissone	149
Skate	155
Slides	158
Social Dance	11
Sous-Sus	49
Soutenu turn	190
Spanish walk	142
Spine protection	58, 231
Spiral turn	190
Split floor series	177
Split slide series	174
Splits	38, 70
Spotting (turns)	180
Stag leap	165
Step touches	135
Stretching	222
Sugar Foot	152
Sur le cou-de-pied position	202
Suzy Q	153
Swastika	38
Swedish fall	170

T

Tap dance	11
Tap lunges	135
Tap walk	134
Teaching different levels	235
Tendu	107
Themes	206
Three step turn	182
Time requirements	13
Tourjete	164
Traveling kicks	144
Traveling turns	144
Turns	180
Turn in the air	194
Twist kick walk	144

U

Uncle Wiggily	154

V

Varsity drag	154

W

Warming up	58
Wishful thinking	210

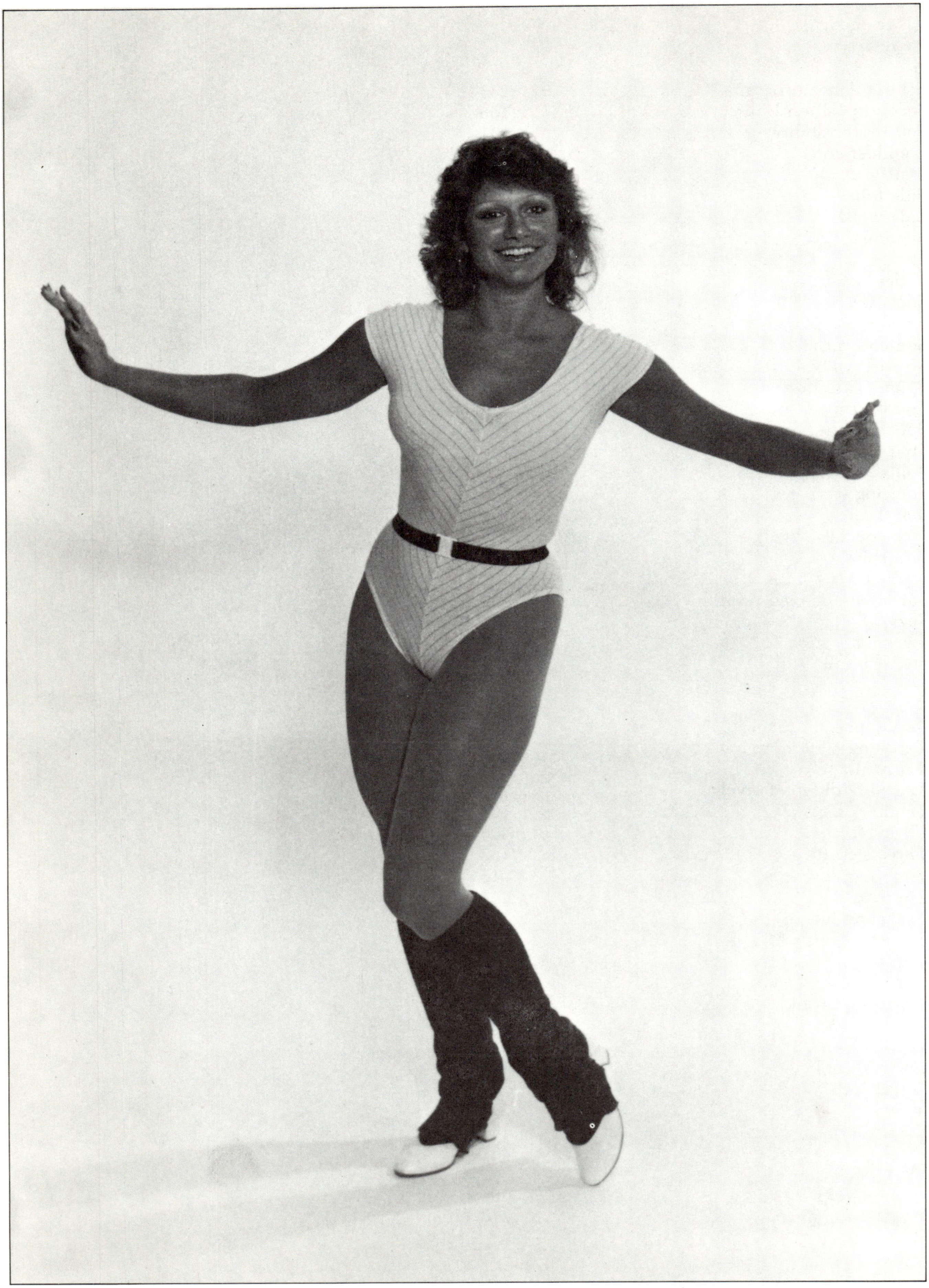